THE

ENGLAND FOOTBALL

MISCELLANY

I would like to dedicate this book to my wife, Janice,
and our two sons, Marc and Paul.

Without them, I am nothing.

With all my love.

John

This edition published in 2006

Copyright © Carlton Books Limited 2006

Carlton Books Limited
20 Mortimer Street
London W1T 3JW

A CIP catalogue record for this book is available from the British Library

ISBN 13: 978-1-86200-366-8
ISBN 10: 1-86200-366-1

Editor: Martin Corteel
Project Art Editor: Darren Jordan
Production: Lisa French

Printed in Great Britain

THE

ENGLAND FOOTBALL

MISCELLANY

JOHN WHITE
WITH A FOREWORD BY GARY LINEKER, OBE

SEVENOAKS

⊞

⟶ AUTHOR'S ACKNOWLEDGEMENTS ⟵

Jan Alsos, Webmaster at www.planetworldcup.com *(for help with World Cup Results & Squads)* ❖ John and Sharon Astill at www.englandfc.com *(for help on many topics)* ❖ Ivan Barnsley at the Birmingham City Historical Society *(for help with the Birmingham City England XI)* ❖ Phil Beeton and Raymond Fell *(for help with the Leeds United England XI)* ❖ Danny Callaghan *(for help with the Newcastle United England XI)* ❖ Bill Clarkson *(for all his help and wisdom)* ❖ Richard Conway *(for help with the Blackburn Rovers England XI)* ❖ Gavin at www.thewolvessite.co.uk *(for help with the Wolverhampton Wanderers England XI)* ❖ Adrian Dearnaley (landlord of The Waggon, Uppermill) ❖ John Dempsey (Carryduff MUSC) ❖ Frankie "Dodger" Dodds ❖ Martin Ferguson (Carryduff MUSC) ❖ Damien Friel (Carryduff MUSC) ❖ Steve Goldby at www.comeonboro.com ❖ Chris Goodwin ❖ Harry the Webmaster at www.englandfanzine.co.uk ❖ Svenn Hanssen *(for help with the Manchester City England XI)* ❖ Kelly Hart *(for help with the Nottingham Forest England XI)* ❖ Steve Hughes at the *Bolton Evening News* ❖ Dale Hurman at www.anzowls.com *(for help with the Sheffield Wednesday England XI)* ❖ The Inns Society www.bjcurtis.force9.co.uk ❖ Glen Isherwood ❖ Darren Jordan *(for his dedication and skill designing the book)* ❖ Diana Law (Manchester United FC) ❖ Keith Legg at www.saintsforever.com *(for help with the Southampton England XI)* ❖ Gary Lineker *(for his foreword to the book)* ❖ Stephen McMenemy (Carryduff MUSC) ❖ Phil Matcham (Official UK Charts Company) ❖ Ralph Morris *(for help with the Ipswich Town England XI and other entries)* ❖ Michael Morrision (Carryduff MUSC) ❖ Matthew Paton at Christie's Auctions ❖ Steve Rigden at www.phespirit.info ❖ David Roberts (Guinness Publishing Limited) ❖ Richard Rosenfeld ❖ Mark Sainsbury *(for help with the Middlesbrough England XI)* ❖ Wilson Steele (Carryduff MUSC) ❖ The Webmaster at www. englandfanzine.co.uk ❖ Steve Westby *(for help with the Notts County England XI)* ❖ Janice White ❖ Marc White ❖ Paul White ❖ Peter Young at www.englandfootballonline.com and Sir Bobby Charlton, Sir Tom Finney, Nat Lofthouse, Bryan Robson, Sir Bobby Robson and Wayne Rooney *(for their kind endorsements for the book)*.

⌒ FOREWORD BY GARY LINEKER ⌒

When I was a young boy growing up in Leicester during the 1960s I was like all other boys at the time, football crazy. I would play football on my way to school, at lunchtime with my mates and after school. Although I was just five-years old at the time, my most cherished England memory is, without doubt, the 1966 World Cup Final when we beat West Germany 4–2 in extra time to win the Jules Rimet Trophy and be crowned world champions. I can still see Nobby Stiles of Manchester United doing a victory jig in the late afternoon sunshine. Those memories are mine to keep forever, and yours to look back on and enjoy.

And so to my own England career. I will always remember my first appearance for my country. I was a Leicester City player at the time, and we played Scotland at Hampden Park on 26 May 1984 in a British Home International Championship game. I came on as a substitute for Tony Woodcock in a 1–1 draw, and I was very honoured to have been given a further 79 caps by my country. I would have loved to have equalled the legendary Sir Bobby Charlton's England goalscoring record of 49 international goals, but will look back fondly on the 48 I was lucky enough to score. And to all those players I played alongside for my country, I would just like to say a special thank you to each and every one of you for your camaraderie. We went through a lot together but I wouldn't change any of it, well apart from the infamous "Hand of God" goal!

Today I am like many others, an avid England fan who wants us to repeat the success of 1966. I am very much looking forward to this summer's World Cup finals in Germany. I know the team we send over there will give a very good account of themselves.

As a proud Englishman, I was delighted when John asked me if I would write the foreword for his book. It is packed with interesting facts, stories, records, statistics and events from when England played an official match for the first time in Glasgow on 25 November 1872, drawing 0–0 with Scotland, right up to the qualification for the 2006 World Cup finals in Germany. And so here you have it, 133 years of our international team's history in one delightful book.

Gary Lineker, OBE (England 1984–1992)
February 2006

∽ LIST OF ABBREVIATIONS ∾

⤚ INTRODUCTION ⤙

There are many people to whom I'd like to give special thanks. Chris Goodwin, Glen Isherwood and Peter Young gave invaluable help on statistics, tables, pieces of trivia and quirky facts, as did their superb website www.englandfootballonline.com, and extra gratitude to Chris for proofreading my work. John and Sharon Astill at www.englandfc.com were an informative guide on numerous subjects, particularly England's opponents and goalscorers. If you are looking up any information on the England national team then look no further than these two websites which, with www.englandfanzine.co.uk, are the definitive guide to the history of the England football team. My thanks also to Matthew Paton at Christie's for his assistance with information relating to items of England football memorabilia sold at Christie's Auctions, and most of all to thanks to my publisher, Martin Corteel, for his help and advice. This book is my second collaboration with Martin and the Carlton Publishing Group, and follows *The Official Manchester United Miscellany*.

And to you, the reader, I hope you enjoy this book as much as I enjoyed compiling it. We can all remember many great England games and special moments from international matches down the years, and I have tried to capture as many of these moments as possible. My book isn't exclusively a collection of trivia or a statistical handbook or indeed a reference guide. It is a combination of all three. The entries date back to England's first ever international match and end with England's qualification for the 2006 World Cup finals in Germany.

I hope my book helps further your knowledge of the England football team, the internationals, the managers and, of course, the many famous players who have pulled on the shirt emblazoned with the three lions. And finally, I hope that I'll have surprised you at least once with one of the many extraordinary entries.

Yours in sport,
John White

⚜

∽ TOP ENGLAND GOALSCORERS ∽

Player	Teams	Goals	Games
Bobby Charlton	Man Utd, 1958–70	49	106
Gary Lineker	Leicester City, Everton, Barcelona, Spurs, 1984–92	48	80
Jimmy Greaves	Chelsea, Spurs, 1959–67	44	57
Michael Owen[†]	Liverpool, Real Madrid, 1998–present	35	75
Nat Lofthouse	Bolton Wanderers, 1951–59	30	33
Alan Shearer	Southampton, Blackburn Rovers, Newcastle Utd, 1992–2000	30	63
Tom Finney	Preston North End, 1947–59	30	76
Vivian Woodward	Spurs, Chelsea, 1903–11	29	23
Steve Bloomer	Derby County, Middlesbrough, 1895–1907	28	23
David Platt	Aston Villa, Bari, Juventus, Sampdoria, Arsenal, 1990–96	27	62
Bryan Robson	WBA, Man Utd, 1980–92	26	90
Geoff Hurst	West Ham, 1966–72	24	49
Stan Mortensen	Blackpool, 1947–54	23	25
Tommy Lawton	Everton, Chelsea, Notts County, 1939–49	22	23
Mick Channon	Southampton, Man City, 1972–77	21	46

∽ THE LIONS ROAR (1) ∽

"You've beaten them once. Now go out and bloody beat them again."
Alf Ramsey to his England team just before the start of extra-time in the 1966 World Cup Final.

∽ ENGLAND'S CENTURIONS ∽

To date there are only four players who have won 100 or more caps for England:

125	Peter Shilton	1970–1990
108	Bobby Moore	1962–1973
106	Bobby Charlton	1958–1970
105	Billy Wright	1946–1959

[†]*Michael Owen's hat-trick in England's 3–2 win over Colombia in New Jersey, USA, on 31 May 2005 moved him from joint seventh to fourth in the list of all-time England goalscorers. Owen has now scored 35 goals, including the two goals he got against Argentina on 12 November 2005.*

⚓ ENGLAND'S LAST 10 CLARETS ⚓

Player	Years
Billy Elliott	1952
Brian Pilkington	1954
Colin McDonald	1958
John Connelly	1959–63
John Angus	1961
George Miller	1961
Ray Pointer	1961
Gordon Harris	1966
Ralph Coates	1970
Martin Dobson	1974

Did You Know That?
Two Burnley players have started at the same time for England on 10 different occasions between 1922 and 1961. The last pairing was Ray Pointer and John Connelly, who played in England's 2–0 win over Portugal at Wembley on 25 October 1961, a game in which both players scored. A total of 24 Burnley players have been capped by England.

⚓ MARCHING ORDERS ⚓

Alan Mullery	v Yugoslavia	Florence on 5 June1968
Alan Ball	v Poland	Chorzow on 6 June 1973
Trevor Cherry	v Argentina	Buenos Aires on 12 June 1977
Ray Wilkins	v Morocco	Monterrey on 6 June 1986
David Beckham	v Argentina	St Etienne on 30 June 30 1998
Paul Ince	v Sweden	Stockholm on 5 September 1998 [†]
Paul Scholes	v Sweden	Wembley on 5 June 1999 [††]
David Batty	v Poland	Warsaw on 8 September 1999
Alan Smith	v Macedonia	Southampton on 16 October 2002
David Beckham	v Austria	Old Trafford on 8 October 2005

⚓ MOST CONSECUTIVE GOALS ⚓

The record for the most consecutive goals scored for England is held by Steve Bloomer who scored in 10 successive appearances (19 goals) between 9 March 1895 (v Ireland) and 20 March 1899 (v Wales).

[†]*This was the first time players were sent off in consecutive internationals for England.*
[††]*Scholes was the first England player to be sent off on English soil.*

⌐ ENGLAND MANAGERS ⌐

Manager	Period
Football Association	30.11.1872 – 24.05.1939
Walter Winterbottom	28.09.1946 – 21.11.1962
Alf Ramsey	27.02.1963 – 03.04.1974
Joe Mercer	11.05.1974 – 05.06.1974
Donald Revie	04.07.1974 – 12.07.1977
Ron Greenwood	07.09.1977 – 05.07.1982
Bobby Robson	22.09.1982 – 07.07.1990
Graham Taylor	12.09.1990 – 17.11.1993
Terry Venables	09.03.1994 – 26.06.1996
Glenn Hoddle	01.09.1996 – 18.11.1998
Howard Wilkinson	01.02.1999 & 11.10.2000
Kevin Keegan	27.03.1999 – 07.10.2000
Peter Taylor	15.11.2000
Sven-Goran Eriksson	12.01.2001 – present

⌐ IRELAND BEAT ENGLAND'S BEST ⌐

When England arrived in Belfast for their British Home International Championship game against Ireland on 15 February 1913, the side was generally regarded as the "best England had ever sent across the Irish Sea". Sunderland's Charlie Buchan made his international debut in the game and scored after just ten minutes to put England 1–0 up. Shortly afterwards Ireland's inside-left, James McAuley of Huddersfield Town, badly injured his knee and was forced to leave the field of play. However, the plucky Irish played on with 10 men and scored twice through their Sheffield United centre-forward, Billy Gillespie. Three minutes from time the referee blew his whistle for a free-kick, and the crowd thought it was the final whistle. The spectators took to the pitch and carried their Irish heroes off shoulder-high. The referee was unable to re-start the game and, remarkably, the result stood. It was Ireland's first ever victory over England.

⌐ FASTEST INTERNATIONAL HAT-TRICK ⌐

The fastest England hat-trick was scored in 3½ minutes by Willie Hall versus Ireland at Old Trafford on 16 November 1938.

⌐ ENGLAND'S SAMPDORIA BRIGADE ⌐

Trevor Francis ❖ David Platt ❖ Des Walker

⚜

⟶ FORMIDABLE HOSTS ⟵

England has hosted one World Cup finals (1966), and one European Championship finals (1996), and they have yet to be beaten on home soil in major finals tournament play. England won the World Cup in 1966, going through the competition unbeaten in six games. In 1996 England failed to advance past the semi-final stages of the European Championship, but they went out of the tournament in a penalty shoot-out, having drawn 1–1 with Germany after extra time.

England have lost only six preliminary games on home soil in major tournaments, four European Championship matches and two World Cup matches. In European Championship qualifying games, Scotland have recorded two victories in England (once in a qualification group match and once in an inter-group play-off match), while West Germany and Denmark won one game each. In World Cup qualifying games, Italy and Germany have each beaten England once on English soil.

⟶ SIX FROM SIX ⟵

Paul Mariner scored in six consecutive games he played for England between 18 November 1982 and 20 June 1982. England's opponents were Hungary, Holland, Scotland, Finland, France and Czechoslovakia.

⟶ SIR ALF'S LAST LINE-UP ⟵

On 3 April 1974 Sir Alf Ramsey took charge of England for the last time, the game with Portugal in Lisbon ending in a 0–0 draw. The team lined up as follows:

1.	Phil Parkes	Queens Park Rangers
2.	David Nish	Derby County
3.	Mike Pejic	Stoke City
4.	Martin Dobson	Burnley
5.	Dave Watson	Sunderland
6.	Colin Todd	Derby County
7.	Stan Bowles	Queens Park Rangers
8.	Mick Channon	Southampton
9.	Malcolm Macdonald	Newcastle United
10.	Trevor Brooking	West Ham United
11.	Martin Peters *(captain)*	Tottenham Hotspur

Sub: Alan Ball *(Arsenal) for Macdonald*

⚜

~ ALAN SHEARER, OBE ~

Alan Shearer was born in Newcastle-upon-Tyne on 13 August 1970. When he was 16-years-old at the famous Wallsend Boys Club, Alan was rejected by Newcastle United. Instead the young striker signed for Southampton as an apprentice. In 1988 he made his Southampton debut as a substitute in a game against Chelsea, and a month later he scored a hat-trick in his full debut, against Arsenal. At 17 years and 8 months old, he'd broken Jimmy Greaves' 30-year record as the youngest player to score a hat-trick in top flight football in England.

On 19 February 1992, Graham Taylor awarded Shearer his first full cap and he scored on his international debut against France at Wembley in a 2–0 win, and was a member of the England squad that qualified for that year's European Championship in Sweden. In 1992, he left the Saints and signed for Blackburn Rovers in what, at the time, was a £3.6 million British record transfer fee. It was at Ewood Park that he won his only major club honour in the game, the Premier League title in 1995. At the end of Blackburn's 1994–95 Championship winning season he was voted the PFA Player of the Year, and was honoured with the same award by his peers two years later.

At the 1996 European Championship, he won the competition's Golden Boot with five goals and he helped England qualify for the 1998 World Cup finals. In 1999, Kevin Keegan made Shearer the England captain such was his importance to the team. Under Keegan, Shearer was an ever-present in the England side that qualified for the 2000 European Championship. Despite heading England's winner against Germany at the finals, England were knocked out of the tournament following defeats to Portugal and Romania. In the 3–2 loss to Romania in Charleroi, Alan scored his last goal for England in his final appearance for his country. In total, he scored 30 times for England in 63 internationals.

During the summer of 1996, his home-town club, Newcastle United, paid a then world record £15 million to Blackburn Rovers to secure his services. On 18 January 2003, Alan scored a goal after only 10 seconds for Newcastle United against Manchester City, equalling the fastest ever goal scored in the Premier League, and also equalling the record for the fastest ever goal scored by a Newcastle United player (Jackie Milburn's strike in November 1947). At the end of the 2004–05 season, Alan had scored a career total of 365 goals and on 4 February 2006, he scored his 201st goal for the Geordies to beat Jackie Milburn's club record of 200.

⚜ ENGLAND'S LAST 10 WOLVES ⚜

Player	Years
Ron Flowers	1955–56
Eddie Clamp	1958
Peter Broadbent	1958–60
Norman Deeley	1959
Chris Crowe	1962
Alan Hinton	1962
Bobby Thomson	1963–64
John Richards	1973
Emlyn Hughes	1980
Steve Bull	1989–90

Did You Know That?
Four Wolverhampton Wanderers players, Billy Wright, Bert Williams, Ron Flowers and Dennis Wishaw, all started for England against France on 15 May 1955 when England lost 1–0 in Paris. Another four, Billy Wright, Ron Flowers, Norman Deeley and Peter Broadbent, started against Brazil in Rio de Janeiro on 13 May 1959, when England lost 2–0. A total of 33 Wolves players have been capped by England.

⚜ ON TARGET AGAINST BRAZIL ⚜

The last 10 England players to score against Brazil are:

Michael Owen	Shizouka	21 June 2002
Michael Owen	Wembley	27 May 2000
Graham Le Saux	Wembley	11 June 1995
David Platt	Washington	13 June 1993
David Platt	Washington	17 May 1992
Gary Lineker	Wembley	28 March 1990
Gary Lineker	Wembley	19 May 1987
Mark Hateley	Rio de Janeiro	10 June 1984
John Barnes	Rio de Janeiro	10 June 1984
Kevin Keegan	Wembley	19 April 1978

⚜ LONGEST NAME ON THE TEAMSHEET ⚜

The longest surname of a player capped by England at full international level – Wingfield-Stratford – has 18 letters. Cecil Vernon Wingfield-Stratford, of the Royal Engineers, played one game for England on 3 March 1877 in a 3–1 defeat at the Kennington Oval.

⤚ WORLD CUP FINALS – BRAZIL 1950 ⤙

England's first World Cup participation came in 1950 when the finals were held in Brazil. England were drawn in Group 2 for the first phase games with Chile, Spain and the USA. England won their opening game 2–0 on 5 June against Chile. Four days later one of the biggest World Cup shocks in history took place when the USA sensationally beat England 1–0 in Estádio Independencia, Belo Horizonte. England lost their final group game 1–0 to the group winners, Spain, in the magnificent Estádio Maracanã, Rio de Janeiro. England finished runners-up in the group which was not good enough to see them progress to the next stage. Uruguay broke the hearts of the home crowds when they beat Brazil 2–1 in the Final in Estádio Maracanã, Rio de Janeiro in front of 202,772 fans. The 1950 World Cup finals was the first time the tournament was not decided by a knock-out final, and it was also the first time that the trophy itself was named "the Jules Rimet Cup" in honour the famous FIFA official.

FIRST ROUND, GROUP 2

25 JUNE 1950, RIO DE JANEIRO, 30,000

England (1) 2   v   **Chile** (0) 0
(Mortensen 27,
Mannion 51)

England: Williams, Ramsey, Aston, Wright, Hughes, Dickinson, Finney, Bentley, Mannion, Mortensen, Mullen.

---

29 JUNE 1950, BELO HORIZONTE, 10,000

USA (1) 1   v   **England** (0) 0
(Gaetjens 38)

England: Williams, Ramsey, Aston, Wright, Hughes, Dickinson, Finney, Bentley, Mannion, Mortensen, Mullen.

---

2 JULY 1950, RIO DE JANEIRO, 74,000

Spain (0) 1   v   **England** (0) 0
(Zarra 48)

England: Williams, Ramsey, Eckersley, Hughes, Wright, Dickinson, Matthews, Baily, Milburn, Mannion, Mortensen.

Group 2 – Final table

	P	W	D	L	F	A	Pts
Spain	3	3	0	0	6	1	6
England	3	1	0	2	2	2	2
Chile	3	1	0	2	5	6	2
USA	3	1	0	2	4	8	2

Winners only qualified for final group stage.

England's 1950 World Cup Finals Squad

John Aston	*(Man Utd)*	Jackie Milburn	*(Newcastle Utd)*
Eddie Bailey	*(Spurs)*	Stan Mortensen	*(Blackpool)*
Roy Bentley	*(Chelsea)*	James Mullen	*(Wolves)*
Henry Cockburn	*(Man Utd)*	Bill Nicholson	*(Spurs)*
James Dickinson	*(Portsmouth)*	Alf Ramsey	*(Spurs)*
Ted Ditchburn	*(Spurs)*	Lawrence Scott	*(Arsenal)*
William Eckersley	*(Blackburn)*	James Taylor	*(Fulham)*
Tom Finney	*(Preston North End)*	William Watson	*(Sunderland)*
Lawrence Hughes	*(Liverpool)*	Bert Williams	*(Wolves)*
Wilf Mannion	*(Middlesbrough)*	Billy Wright	*(Wolves)*
Stanley Matthews	*(Blackpool)*		

Manager: Walter Winterbottom

Did You Know That?

Squad numbers were not required until the 1950 World Cup finals. The players wore numbers 1 to 11. No substitutions were permitted for any reason during the tournament.

⟋ BRITISH PRISONER OF WAR ⟍

Steve Bloomer, who scored 28 times in 23 matches for England between 9 March 1895 and 6 April 1907, retired in 1914. Bloomer moved to Germany in 1914 and took up his new job as a football coach. However, when World War I began in 1914, Bloomer, along with several other British footballers, was interned in the Ruhleben Prison Camp for the duration of the war. Bloomer set up a "Football Association" inside the camp, and the prisoners played a football match every day on a nearby racecourse.

⟋ GAY PLAYS FOR ENGLAND ⟍

Leslie Gay played in goal three times for England. He made his debut on 1 April 1893 in a 5–2 win over Scotland as a Cambridge University player. His next two caps were won as an Old Brightonians player.

⚜ ENGLAND XI – MANCHESTER UNITED ⚜

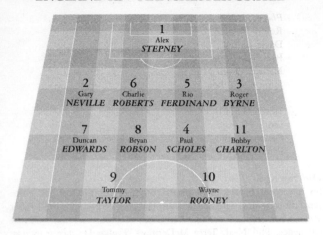

1
Alex
STEPNEY

2
Gary
NEVILLE

6
Charlie
ROBERTS

5
Rio
FERDINAND

3
Roger
BYRNE

7
Duncan
EDWARDS

8
Bryan
ROBSON

4
Paul
SCHOLES

11
Bobby
CHARLTON

9
Tommy
TAYLOR

10
Wayne
ROONEY

Substitutes
Gary *BAILEY*, Paul *PARKER*, Ray *WILKINS*,
Steve *COPPELL*, Jack *ROWLEY*
Manager
Walter *WINTERBOTTOM*

Did You Know That?

Manchester United began life as Newton Heath in 1878 when a group of workers from the Lancashire & Yorkshire Railways formed a football team. Newton Heath takes its name from the old English meaning "the new town on the heath". In the early days the players used the nearby pub, the Three Crowns Inn, for changing facilities.

⚜ THE LIONS ROAR (2) ⚜

"It wasn't the 'Hand of God'. It was the hand of a rascal. God had nothing to do with it."
England manager **Bobby Robson** *rejects the notion of divine intervention in Maradona's first goal for Argentina in the quarter-finals of the 1986 World Cup finals.*

⚜ ENGLAND'S RECORD WIN ⚜

England 13 Ireland 0 – Belfast, 18 February 1882

~ ENGLAND'S LAST 10 MERSEY REDS ~

Player	Years
Robbie Fowler	1996–2001
David James	1997
Paul Ince	1997–99
Michael Owen	1998–2004
Jamie Carragher	1999–2005
Nick Barmby	2000–01
Steven Gerrard	2000–05
Emile Heskey	2000–04
Danny Murphy	2001–03
Peter Crouch	2005–

Did You Know That?
Six Liverpool players have played together for England on three separate occasions. The first was against Switzerland on 7 September 1977, when England manager Ron Greenwood picked goalkeeper Ray Clemence, Phil Neal, Terry McDermott, Emlyn Hughes (captain), Ray Kennedy and Ian Callaghan. A total of 56 Liverpool players have been capped by England.

~ HALF-CENTURY FOR BECKHAM ~

David Beckham captained England for the 50th time in his career when England played Argentina in a friendly in Geneva, Switzerland, on 12 November 2005. Chelsea's Hernan Crespo opened the scoring for the Argentineans before Manchester United's Wayne Rooney scored his 11th goal for his country to bring the sides level. Walter Samuel scored a second half goal to nudge Argentina ahead in his 50th appearance for his country, but Michael Owen scored twice in stoppage time to give England a 3-2 win. Owen had now scored 35 goals in 75 appearances for England.

~ SVEN'S PROTÉGÉS ~

Here are some players who won their first international cap for England under Sven-Goran Eriksson:

James Beattie ❖ Lee Bowyer ❖ Wayne Bridge ❖ Michael Carrick
Ashley Cole ❖ Joe Cole ❖ Owen Hargreaves ❖ Jermain Jenas
Ledley King ❖ Danny Murphy ❖ Paul Robinson ❖ Wayne Rooney
Alan Smith ❖ John Terry ❖ Darius Vassell ❖ Peter Crouch

✠

⤳ LOYAL SERVANTS ⤳

Stanley Matthews played for England for 23 years, making his first international appearance on 29 September 1934 and his last on 15 May 1957.

Peter Shilton played for England for over 20 years. He made his debut on 25 November 1970 and made his final appearance for England on 7 July 1990. However, whereas Matthews won 54 caps and did not make any international appearances in 1936, or from 1940 to 1946, because of the war, Shilton made 125 appearances and only missed a cap in one year, 1976.

⤳ SING YOUR HEARTS OUT FOR THE LADS ⤳

The England World Cup Squad have made a number of notable forays into the world of pop music. These are the chartbusters from the aspiring net-busters:

England World Cup Squad
UK, male football team vocalists (46 WEEKS IN THE CHARTS)   *pos/wks*

18 Apr 70 *	**Back Home** *Pye 7N 17920*		1 16
15 Aug 70	**Back Home** *(re-entry) Pye 7N 17920*		46 1
10 Apr 82 •	**This Time (We'll Get It Right)/**		
	England We'll Fly The Flag *England ER1*		2 13
18 Apr 86	**We've Got The Whole World At Our Feet/**		
	When We Are Far From Home		
	Columbia DB 9128		66 2
21 May 88	**All The Way** *MCA GOAL 1*	1	64 2
2 Jun 90 *	**World In Motion**		
	Factory/MCA FAC 2937	2	1 12

UK No.1 *   UK Top 10 •

1 England Football Team and the 'sound' of Stock, Aitken and Waterman
2 Englandneworder

Courtesy of *The Book of British Hit Singles & Albums* by Guinness World Records and the UK Charts Company

⤳ ENGLAND TEAM SPONSORS 2005–06 ⤳

Carlsberg ✤ McDonald's ✤ Nationwide ✤ Pepsi ✤ Umbro

✠

⌁ WHERE THEY CAME FROM ⌁

The following teams all provided England internationals during the nineteenth century:

1st Surrey Rifles ✢ Barnes ✢ Birmingham Excelsior
Cambridge University ✢ Clapham Rovers ✢ Harrow Chequers
Hendon ✢ Hertfordshire Rangers ✢ Old Carthusians
Old Etonians ✢ Old Harrovians ✢ Owlerton ✢ Oxford University
Pilgrims ✢ Royal Engineers ✢ Saltley College ✢ Shropshire Wanderers
✢ Swifts ✢ Thursday Wanderers ✢ Upton Park ✢ Weybridge
Uxbridge ✢ Wanderers ✢ Wednesday Old Athletic

⌁ ONE GOAL EVERY 0.33 GAMES ⌁

Five players scored a hat-trick on their only England appearance, giving them all a record of scoring a goal every 0.33 games:

Albert Allen (*Aston Villa*) v Ireland on 31 March 1888
John Yates (*Burnley*) v Ireland on 2 March 1889
Walter Gilliat (*Old Carthusians*) v Ireland on 25 February 1893
John Veitch (*Old Westminsters*) v Wales on 12 March 1894
Francis Bradshaw (*Sheffield Wed*) v Austria on 8 June 1908

⌁ BIG THREE MISSING ⌁

Up to the end of the 2004–05 season, the last time England played a full international without a single player from Arsenal, Liverpool or Manchester United in the starting line-up was against France in Malmo on 14 June 1992. The team was as follows:

1. Chris Woods.............................(Sheffield Wednesday)
2. Andy Sinton...............................(Queens Park Rangers)
3. Stuart Pearce.............................(Nottingham Forest)
4. Martin Keown..............................(Everton)
5. Des Walker.................................(Nottingham Forest)
6. Carlton Palmer..........................(Sheffield Wednesday)
7. David Platt.................................(Bari)
8. David Batty................................(Leeds United)
9. Alan Shearer.............................(Southampton)
10. Gary Lineker............................(Tottenham Hotspur)
11. Trevor Steven...........................(Olympique Marseille)
The game finished 0–0.

✠

⟶ IF THE CAP FITS ⟶

The first England international cap was made of royal blue velvet, with a red rose at the front and the date of the match on the peak. Some years later the initial letter of the opposing country, e.g. "I" for Ireland, was added on the peak. Then a silver tassle was added and, finally, the red rose was replaced by the three lions. Today the England international caps are still made from blue velvet and are supplied to the Football Association by the Midlands-based company, Toye, Kenning & Spencer.

⟶ ENGLAND'S GOLDEN OLDIES ⟶

Player	Age
Sir Stanley Matthews	42 years, 104 days
Peter Shilton	40 years, 292 days
Alexander Morten	40 years, 67 days
Frank Osbourne	39 years, 221 days
Edward Taylor	39 years, 40 days
David Seaman	39 years, 27 days
Leslie Compton	38 years, 70 days
Stuart Pearce	37 years, 137 days
Jesse Pennington	36 years, 230 days
Sam Hardy	36 years, 227 days

⟶ SIX SAINTLY ENGLAND CAPTAINS ⟶

The following six players all played for Southampton during their careers and also captained England:

Alan Ball ❖ Mick Channon ❖ Kevin Keegan ❖ Mick Mills
Peter Shilton ❖ Dave Watson

⟶ THREE DECADES OF SERVICE ⟶

Since the end of the World War II, five players have played for England in three different decades:

Bobby Charlton	1950s, 1960s and 1970s
Emlyn Hughes	1960s, 1970s and 1980s
Peter Shilton	1970s, 1980s and 1990s
Tony Adams	1980s, 1990s and 2000s
David Seaman	1980s, 1990s and 2000s

⚜

⚓ THE BATTLE OF HIGHBURY ⚓

In 1934 England and Italy were regarded by many as the two best teams in the world. For this friendly international, England fielded seven Arsenal players with the match being played at their club ground, Arsenal Stadium (Highbury). Early in the game an Italian player was taken off injured and, with no substitutes permitted in the 1930s, the Italians had to play the remainder of the game with 10 men. Italy set about England and turned the first 45 minutes into a war. Several of the home players were badly injured, one suffering a broken arm and another a broken nose. At the interval, England led 3–0, and a more subdued Italy pulled two goals back in the second half. Many of the England players claimed it was the dirtiest game they'd ever played in – hence it became known in football folklore as "The Battle of Highbury".

England: Frank Moss (*Arsenal*), George Male (*Arsenal*), Eddie Hapgood (*Arsenal*), Cliff Britton (*Everton*), John Barker (*Derby County*), Wilf Copping (*Arsenal*), Stanley Matthews (*Stoke City*), Ray Bowden (*Arsenal*), Ted Drake (*Arsenal*), Cliff Bastin (*Arsenal*), Eric Brook (*Man City*).

⚓ MOST GOALS IN A GAME ⚓

The most goals scored by a player in one game for England:

(5) Oliver Vaughton v Ireland ....Belfast, 18 February 1882
(5) Steve Bloomer v Wales ....Cardiff, 16 March 1896
(5) Willie Hall v Ireland ....Old Trafford, 16 November 1938
(5) Malcolm Macdonald v Cyprus ....Wembley, 16 April 1975

⚓ PENALTY SHOOT-OUT FALLGUYS ⚓

1990 World Cup – Stuart Pearce and Chris Waddle missed against Germany; Euro 96 – Gareth Southgate missed against Germany; 1998 King Hassan II Cup – Rob Lee and Les Ferdinand missed against Belgium; 1998 World Cup – Paul Ince and David Batty missed against Argentina; Euro 2004 – David Beckham and Darius Vassell missed against Portugal.

England lost all five of these penalty shoot-outs. The only time they won a penalty shoot-out was in their Euro 96 quarter-final encounter with Spain at Wembley. The score was 4–2. (Spain missed two penalties, so England did not need to take a fifth one.)

↞ SIR ALF RAMSEY ↠

Alfred Ramsey was born on 22 January 1920 in Dagenham, Essex. In 1946 he made his first team debut for Southampton, a club he joined just after the end of World War II. Alf won his first England cap in a friendly against Switzerland at Arsenal Stadium on 1 December 1948 which England won 6–0. He went on to win a total of 32 caps for England, 29 in succession, scoring three penalties. In 1949, Tottenham Hotspur paid £29,000 to take him to White Hart Lane, and he became a member of the famous Spurs "push and run" side that won the English Second and First Divisions in successive seasons in 1950 and 1951.

In 1955, Alf hung up his boots and took his first step into management. His first job was as manager of Ipswich Town, a club he took from Division 3 to Division 1 in just six seasons. In their first season in the First Division, in 1961–62, the unfashionable Suffolk club stunned English football by winning the Championship. Ironically, by virtue of Ipswich's championship success he emulated, as a manager, the feat he achieved as a player, by wining successive Second and First Division championships.

Alf Ramsey was not the FA's first choice to succeed Walter Winterbottom as the England manager in 1963. The job was first offered to Jimmy Adamson, Winterbottom's assistant, but Adamson turned the invitation down and Ramsey was appointed. Things did not get off to a good start for Ramsey. In his first game in charge, England travelled to Paris on 27 February 1963 where they lost 5–2 to the French in a European Championship qualifying game. Bobby Smith and Bobby Tambling scored for England. Alf's greatest moment came in 1966, when he managed England to a dramatic 4–2 World Cup Final win over West Germany at Wembley after extra-time. In 1967 he was given a knighthood. Sir Alf's last game in charge of England was a 0–0 draw against Portugal in Lisbon on 3 April 1974. So, after 113 games in charge, in which England won more than half of their games, Sir Alf was sacked and Joe Mercer temporarily took charge of England team affairs. Sir Alf died on 28 April 1999.

Did You Know That?
Alf won his 32nd and final cap on 25 November 1953 when Hungary, the Mighty Magyars, beat England 6–3 at Wembley Stadium. Ramsey scored in the game. It was the first time England had lost to a foreign side at the famous stadium.

⟋ ENGLAND'S LAST 10 ADDICKS ᛰ

Player	Years
Harold Miller	1923
George Armitage	1925
Harold Hobbis	1936
Don Welsh	1938–39
Derek Ufton	1953
Mike Bailey	1964–65
Chris Powell	2001–02
Paul Konchesky	2003
Scott Parker	2003
Luke Young	2005

Did You Know That?
England have never fielded two Charlton Athletic players at the same time in a game. However, Scott Parker was an unused substitute when Paul Konchesky won his only England cap in their 3–1 defeat to Australia at Upton Park on 12 February 2003. England used 11 substitutes in the game. A total of 11 Charlton Athletic players have been capped by England up to the end of 2005.

⟋ MATTHEWS–MORTENSEN DUO ᛰ

The Blackpool partnership of Stanley Matthews and Stanley Mortensen also made it into the England starting line-up on 12 occasions from 27 May 1947 to 25 November 1953. Six of the matches were won and two drawn, with Mortensen scoring nine goals to Matthews' one. Their first England game together was a 10–0 win over Portugal in Lisbon, with Mortensen scoring four times and Matthews once. After their last game together, the 6–3 Wembley defeat to Hungary, Mortensen never won another cap whereas Matthews went on to win a further 18 caps.

⟋ 11 TIMES THREE ᛰ

Up to the end of the 2004–05 season, 11 England players have scored a hat-trick in a World Cup qualifying game or World Cup finals game:

Jackie Milburn ✥ Jack Rowley ✥ Tommy Taylor (twice)
Jimmy Greaves ✥ Bobby Charlton ✥ Geoff Hurst ✥ Bryan Robson
Gary Lineker (twice) ✥ David Platt ✥ Ian Wright ✥ Michael Owen

⟡ WORLD CUP FINALS – SWITZERLAND 1954 ⟡

At the 1954 World Cup finals in Switzerland, England were drawn in Group D with Belgium, Italy and the host nation. It was the first time television covered the finals. A new seeding system was also introduced in the group stages where the two teams ranked highest in FIFA's world rankings in each group would not play each other. In their opening game, England drew 4–4 with Belgium after extra-time in the St Jakob Stadion, Basle. Because of the group seeding, each team had to play only two group games and England avoided Italy. In their second game England beat the hosts, Switzerland, 2–0 in the Wankdorf Stadion, Berne. England topped the group with three points. In their quarter-final game England had to confront the holders, Uruguay. England lost 4–2 in the St Jakob Stadion. West Germany beat Hungary 3–2 in the Final, which was played in the Wankdorf Stadion in front of 62,472 fans.

FIRST ROUND, GROUP 4

17 JUNE 1954, BASEL, 40,000

England (2) 4   v   **Belgium** (1) 4
(Broadis 26, 63,   (Anoul 5, 71, Coppens 67,
Lofthouse 36, 91)   (Dickinson o.g. 94)

England lost 4–3 on penalties

England: Merrick, Staniforth, Byrne, Wright, Owen, Dickinson, Matthews, Broadis, Lofthouse, Taylor, Finney.

---

20 JUNE 1954, BERNE, 50,000

England (1) 2   v   **Switzerland** (0) 0
(Mullen 43, Wishaw 69)

England: Merrick, Staniforth, Byrne, Wright, McGarry, Dickinson, Finney, Broadis, Wishaw, Taylor, Mullen.

Group G – Final table

	P	W	D	L	F	A	Pts
England	2	1	1	0	6	4	3
Switzerland*	2	1	0	1	2	3	2
Italy	2	1	0	1	5	3	2
Austria	2	0	1	1	5	8	1

*Switzerland defeated Italy 4–1 in a play-off.

QUARTER-FINAL
26 JUNE 1954, BASLE, 35,000
Uruguay (2) 4   v   England (2) 2
(Borges 5, Varela 39,   (Lofthouse 16, Finney 67)
Schiaffino 46, Ambrois 78)

England: Merrick, Staniforth, Byrne, Wright, McGarry, Dickenson,
Matthews, Broadis, Lofthouse,
Wishaw, Finney.

England's 1954 World Cup Finals Squad

Gil Merrick	*(Birmingham City)*	Stanley Matthews	*(Blackpool)*
Ted Burgin	*(Sheff Utd)*	Ivor Broadis	*(Newcastle Utd)*
Ron Staniforth	*(Huddersfield)*	Nat Lofthouse	*(Bolton)*
Roger Byrne	*(Man Utd)*	Tommy Taylor	*(Man Utd)*
Ken Green	*(Birmingham City)*	Tom Finney	*(Preston North End)*
Billy Wright	*(Wolves)*	Albert Quixall	*(Sheff Wed)*
Sid Owen	*(Luton Town)*	Dennis Wilshaw	*(Wolves)*
Jimmy Dickenson	*(Portsmouth)*	Jimmy Mullen	*(Wolves)*
Bill McGarry	*(Huddersfield)*		

Manager: Walter Winterbottom

Did You Know That?
The 1954 World Cup finals marked the 50th anniversary of the
Federation of International Football Associations (FIFA). FIFA's head
office is based in Geneva, Switzerland. The all-conquering "Magic
Magyars" were the tournament favourites scoring 23 goals on their
way to the Final before falling at the last hurdle to the Germans.

⌁ THE LIONS ROAR (3) ⌁

"England's best football will come against the right type of opposition
– a team who come to play football and not act like animals."
*Alf Ramsey reacting angrily to foul play in the quarter-final against
Argentina in the 1966 World Cup finals.*

⌁ KEEP IT IN THE FAMILY ⌁

Three father-and-son combinations have played for England:

George Eastham Snr and George Eastham Jnr
Brian and Nigel Clough
Frank Lampard Snr and Frank Lampard Jnr

~ ENGLAND XI – SOUTHAMPTON ~

1
Peter
SHILTON

2
Alf
RAMSEY

6
Dave
WATSON

5
Mark
WRIGHT

3
Mick
MILLS

7
Terry
PAINE

8
Kevin
KEEGAN

4
Matt
LE TISSIER

11
Steve
WILLIAMS

9
Alan
SHEARER

10
Mick
CHANNON

Substitutes
Tim *FLOWERS*, Graeme *LE SAUX*, Jamie *REDKNAPP*,
Kevin *PHILIPS*, Peter *CROUCH*
Player-Manager
Sir Alf *RAMSEY*

Did You Know That?

Southampton Football Club began life as St Mary's YMA. The Saints
were formed in November 1885 and occupied The Dell for over
100 years before moving to its existing St Mary's Stadium in 2001.
Southampton's greatest day came in the 1976 FA Cup Final when
they beat Manchester United 1–0.

~ '66 FINAL GOALS TALLY ~

The goals in the 1966 World Cup Final at Wembley were scored
as follows:

Haller, 12	England	0	West Germany	1
Hurst, 18	England	1	West Germany	1
Peters, 78	England	2	West Germany	1
Weber, 89	England	2	West Germany	2
Hurst, 100	England	3	West Germany	2
Hurst, 120	England	4	West Germany	2

⚜

✑ CAPS INTRODUCED ✑

International caps were awarded by the Football Association for the first time in 1886. England's first capped players beat Ireland 6–1 in Belfast on 13 March 1886. The team lined up as follows:

1. William Rose........................Preston North End
2. Percy Walters........................Old Carthusians
3   Richard Baugh........................Stafford Road
4. George Shutt........................Stoke City
5. Ralph Squire........................Cambridge University
6. Charles Dobson........................Notts County
7. John Leighton........................Nottingham Forest
8. Frederick Dewhurst........................Preston North End
9. Tinsley Lindley........................Cambridge University
10. Benjamin Spilsbury........................Cambridge University
11. Thelwell Pike........................Cambridge University

Scorers: Spilsbury 4, Dewhurst & Lindley

✑ THE SHORT AND THE TALL ✑

The smallest player to play for England was Tottenham Hotspur's Frederick "Fanny" Walden[†], who played from 1914 to 1922 and whose height was 5ft 2½in. The tallest for more than 120 years was Notts County's Billy Gunn, who played in 1884 and was 6ft 4¾in tall but then Peter Crouch made his England debut against Colombia on 31 May 2005. Crouch stands 6ft 6in tall.

✑ SCORING AT THE WRONG END ✑

The following is a list of own goals scored by England players since 1945:

Richard Wright v Malta	3 June 2000
Tony Adams v Holland	23 March 1988
Phil Neal v Australia	19 June 1983
Phil Thompson v Wales	17 May 1980
Colin Todd v Scotland	18 May 1974
Jimmy Dickinson v Belgium	17 June 1954
Leslie Compton v Yugoslavia	22 November 1950

[†]*Fanny Walden won two caps for England. He made his debut on 4 April 1914 against Scotland but did not represent England again until 13 March 1922 (against Wales).*

✧ NICKNAMES OF ENGLAND PLAYERS ✧

Beats	James Beattie
Big Al	Alan Shearer
Bite Yer Legs	Norman Hunter
Bogota Bandit	Charlie Mitten
Butch	Ray Wilkins
Crazy Horse	Emlyn Hughes
Fatty	William Foulkes
Gazza	Paul Gascoigne
Golden Balls	David Beckham
Happy	Nobby Stiles
Lion of Vienna	Nat Lofthouse
Merlin	Gordon Hill
Mooro	Bobby Moore
Morty	Stan Mortensen
Nijinsky	Colin Bell
Pancho	Stuart Pearson
Pongo	Thomas Waring
Psycho	Stuart Pearce
Shaggy	Steve McManaman
Sicknote	Darren Anderton
Super Kev	Kevin Keegan
The Cat	Peter Bonetti
The Giraffe	Jackie Charlton
Wizard of the Dribble	Stanley Matthews
Wor Jackie	Jackie Milburn

✧ LUCKY 13 FOR BECKHAM ✧

Up to the end of the 2004–05 season, David Beckham had scored 13 goals for England:

26 June 1998	Colombia	12 October 2002	Slovakia
24 March 2001	Finland	16 October 2002	Macedonia
25 May 2001	Mexico	29 March 2003	Liechtenstein
6 June 2001	Greece	2 April 2003	Turkey
6 October 2001	Greece	20 August 2003	Croatia
10 November 2001	Sweden	6 September 2003	Macedonia
7 June 2002	Argentina		

Did You Know That?
His last 3 goals were all penalties.

⚜

❧ THE GREATEST SAVE EVER ❧

Clive Leatherdale, in his excellent *England: The Quest for the World Cup – A Complete Record (1950–2002)*, writes:

"The eleventh minute was rather special. The 1970 World Cup is remembered for a handful of special moments. Most of them were provided by Brazil – but not this time. Carlos Alberto fed Jairzinho down the right touchline. With an awesome change of pace, the winger accelerated past Cooper to the by-line and swung over a perfect cross. Pele, timing his run to the far post perfectly, rose above Mullery to power a lethal downward header. The Jalisco Stadium acclaimed a goal. So did Pele. But Banks, originally stationed by the opposite post to cover Jairzinho's cross, propelled himself across his goal-line to deflect the ball, as it reared up off the ground, over the cross-bar. It was the finest save that many people had ever seen, securing Banks's ranking amongst the greatest goalkeepers of all time."

❧ TWO GOALS AVERAGE PER CAP ❧

George Camsell won nine caps for England from 9 May 1929 to 9 May 1936. In his nine internationals he scored a remarkable 18 goals, giving him one of the best goals to games played ratios among England's most prolific strikers.

Date	Opponent	Score	Goals
9 May 1929	France	4–1	2 goals
11 May 1929	Belgium	5–1	4 goals
19 October 1929	Ireland	3–0	2 goals
20 November 1929	Wales	6–0	3 goals
6 December 1933	France	4–1	2 goals
4 December 1935	Germany	3–0	2 goals
4 April 1936	Scotland	1–1	1 goal
6 May 1936	Austria	1–2	1 goal
9 May 1936	Belgium	2–3	1 goal

❧ SOLE WEMBLEY VICTORIES ❧

The following national teams all won a single match against England at Wembley:

Austria ❖ Chile ❖ Denmark ❖ France ❖ Holland ❖ Hungary
Spain ❖ Sweden ❖ USSR ❖ Uruguay ❖ Wales

⚓ BACK-TO-BACK WARM-UPS ⚓

On 2 June 1982 England drew 1–1 in Reykjavik with Iceland in a warm-up game for the 1982 World Cup finals. In another friendly the following night England beat Finland 4–1 in Helsinki.[†]

⚓ WALTER'S ONE MANAGEMENT JOB ⚓

Walter Winterbottom[††], who managed England from 1946 to 1962, never managed any other team prior to or after his tenure as the national team manager. Under his leadership England won the British Home International Championships on seven occasions and were joint winners on seven other occasions. England also qualified for every World Cup finals they entered when he was in charge – in 1950, 1954, 1958 and 1962.

⚓ THE START OF SOMETHING BIG ⚓

The England national football team was established in 1870, although they did not play their first official international football match until 1872.[†††] An England national team was first called together for a match against Scotland when the Secretary of the Football Association, Charles W. Alcock, published a letter in *The Sportsman*, a London newspaper, on 5 February 1870. However, severe frost caused the postponement of the match, originally scheduled for 19 February 1870 at the Kennington Oval. The game eventually took place on 5 March 1870 and ended in a 1–1 draw. Later, in 1870, another match between England and Scotland was held, followed by two more in 1871 and a fifth in early 1872. These initial matches were merely informal games, and they are not regarded as official internationals because the Scotland team was made up of London-based Scots together with several "all-comers" to make up the numbers.

⚓ SUPER TOMMY ⚓

Tommy Lawton scored 22 times in 23 appearances for England.

[†]*Steve Perryman of Tottenham Hotspur won his first and only England cap in the game against Iceland.*
[††]*Walter Winterbottom awarded three future England managers their first international caps – Alf Ramsey, Don Revie and Bobby Robson.*
[†††]*The world's first official international football match was held on 30 November 1872 at Hamilton Crescent, Glasgow, and resulted in a scoreless draw between England and Scotland.*

⚜ POPULAR PIERLUIGI COLLINA ⚜

The following England games have been refereed by the accomplished Italian match official:

England	0,	Scotland	1	Wednesday, 17 November 1999
England	1,	Germany	0	Saturday, 17 June 2000
Germany	1,	England	5	Saturday, 1 September 2001
Argentina	0,	England	1	Friday, 7 June 2002
Turkey	0,	England	0	Saturday, 11 October 2003
Croatia	2,	England	4	Monday, 21 June 2004

⚜ ENGLAND'S LAST 10 CITY BLUES ⚜

Player	Years
Joe Corrigan	1976–82
Mick Channon	1977
Peter Barnes	1977–79
Kevin Reeves	1980
Trevor Francis	1981–82
Keith Curle	1992
David White	1992
Trevor Sinclair	2003
David James	2004–05
Shaun Wright-Phillips	2004–05

Did You Know That?
Three Manchester City players have played together for England on three separate occasions. The last was against Brazil on 19 April 1978 in a 1–1 draw at Wembley when Peter Barnes, Joe Corrigan and Dave Watson all played. A total of 36 Manchester City players have been capped by England.

⚜ NEVER BEEN TO WEMBLEY ⚜

A total of 18 national teams that played England elsewhere never played at Wembley. Two of these nations, Bohemia and United Ireland, ceased to exist before Wembley was officially opened. The other 16 nations are:

Australia ❖ C.I.S. ❖ Canada ❖ China ❖ Ecuador ❖ Egypt
Iceland ❖ Israel ❖ Kuwait ❖ Malaysia ❖ Morocco ❖ New Zealand
Paraguay ❖ Peru ❖ South Africa ❖ Tunisia

∽ WORLD CUP FINALS – SWEDEN 1958 ∾

The 1958 World Cup finals were hosted by Sweden. In their opening game played in Göteborg, England drew 2–2 with the USSR. Three days later England drew 0–0 with the 1950 World Cup winners, Brazil, and in their final group game, England drew 2–2 with Austria in the Ryavallen Stadion, Boras. England's three successive draws gave them a share of top place in the group resulting in a play-off match against the USSR to determine which team would progress to the next stage. England lost 1–0 in the Nya Ullevi Stadion. Brazil went on to win the World Cup beating the hosts 5–2 in a pulsating final.

FIRST ROUND, GROUP 4

8 JUNE 1958, GOTHENBURG, 45,000

Soviet Union (1) 2   v   **England** (0) 2
(Simonian 13, Ivanov 55)   (Kevan 66,
                                  Finney (pen) 85)

England: McDonald, Howe, Banks, Clamp, Wright,
Slater, Douglas, Robson, Kevan,
Haynes, Finney.

———————

11 JUNE 1958, GOTHENBURG, 30,000
Brazil (0) 0   v   **England** (0) 0

England: McDonald, Howe, Banks, Clamp, Wright,
Slater, Douglas, Robson, Kevan,
Haynes, A'Court.

———————

15 JUNE 1958, GOTHENBURG, 16,800
England (0) 2   v   **Austria** (2) 2
(Haynes 56, Kevan 73)   (Koller 16, Körner 70)

England: McDonald, Howe, Banks, Clamp, Wright,
Slater, Douglas, Robson, Kevan,
Haynes, A'Court.

———————

Group G – Final table

	P	W	D	L	F	A	Pts
Brazil	3	2	1	0	5	0	5
Soviet Union	3	1	1	1	5	4	3
England	3	0	3	0	4	5	3
Austria	3	0	1	2	2	7	1

PLAY-OFF

17 JUNE 1958, GOTHENBURG, 23,180

Soviet Union (0) 1   v   England (0) 0
(Ilin 68)

England: McDonald, Howe, Banks, Clamp, Wright,
Slater, Broadbent, Robson, Kevan,
Haynes, Finney.

England's 1958 World Cup Finals Squad

1	Colin McDonald *(Burnley)*	12	Eddie Hopkinson *(Bolton)*
2	Don Howe *(WBA)*	13	Alan Hodgkinson* *(Sheff Utd)*
3	Tommy Banks *(Bolton)*	14	Peter Sillett *(Chelsea)*
4	Eddie Clamp *(Wolves)*	15	Ronnie Clayton *(Blackburn)*
5	Billy Wright *(Wolves)*	16	Maurice Norman *(Spurs)*
6	Bill Slater *(Wolves)*	17	Peter Brabrook *(Chelsea)*
7	Bryan Douglas *(Blackburn R)*	18	Peter Broadbent *(Wolves)*
8	Bobby Robson *(WBA)*	19	Bobby Smith *(Spurs)*
9	Derek Kevan *(WBA)*	20	Bobby Charlton *(Man Utd)*
10	Johnny Haynes *(Fulham)*	21	Alan A'Court *(Liverpool)*
11	Tom Finney *(Preston)*	22	Maurice Setters* *(WBA)*

Manager: Walter Winterbottom

*On reserve at home.

Did You Know That?
No substitutions were permitted for any reason during the tournament.

⟿ THE LIONS ROAR (4) ⟿

"I have to admit that I had a bit of sympathy for the Germans. They
genuinely believed the ball had not crossed the line and they may
be right."
*Scorer **Geoff Hurst** muses on the validity of England's third goal in the
1966 World Cup Final.*

⟿ INTERNATIONAL HONOURS ⟿

FIFA World Cup	1966
Olympic Team Gold	1900, 1908 & 1912
British Home International Championships	Winners – 54 times
England Challenge Cup	1991
Le Tournoi de France	1997
The Rous Cup	1986, 1988 & 1989

⟶ POLE AXED ⟵

On 17 October 1973 Poland drew 1–1 with England in a World Cup qualifying game at Wembley. The result meant England could not qualify for the 1974 finals in West Germany.[†] Here is the England team that played that night:

1. Peter Shilton................................Leicester City
2. Paul Madeley................................Leeds United
3. Emlyn Hughes..............................Liverpool
4. Colin Bell.....................................Manchester City
5. Roy McFarland............................Derby County
6. Norman Hunter...........................Leeds United
7. Tony Currie.................................Sheffield United
8. Mick Channon.............................Southampton
9. Martin Chivers...........................Tottenham Hotspur
10. Allan Clarke................................Leeds United
11. Martin Peters (*captain*)...........Tottenham Hotspur
12. Kevin Hector (*for Chivers*)................Derby County
   Scorer: Clarke, pen. 63 mins

⟶ SUCCESSFUL VISITORS TO WEMBLEY ⟵

Only three visiting teams, Chile, Germany and Italy, have winning records against England at Wembley. Chile played there twice, winning one and drawing the other. Italy visited Wembley five times, winning two, drawing two and losing just one. The united Germany team visited Wembley three times and came away with two wins and a draw. (If we include West Germany's results, then the German record at Wembley was four wins, four defeats and one draw.)

⟶ SPORTS PERSONALITY OF THE YEAR ⟵

The following England players have won the coveted BBC Sports Personality of the Year Award:

Bobby Moore.............................1966
Paul Gascoigne.........................1990
Michael Owen............................1998
David Beckham..........................2001

[†] *It was the first time England failed to qualify for a World Cup Finals tournament and eventually led to the sacking of Sir Alf Ramsey.*

✦ SIX CLEAN SHEETS FOR DON ✦

After Don Revie took over as England coach the team not only went unbeaten in their first six games but did it with six clean sheets[†]:

3–0	v	Czechoslovakia	Wembley	30 October 1974
0–0	v	Portugal	Wembley	20 November 1974
2–0	v	West Germany	Wembley	12 March 1975
5–0	v	Cyprus	Wembley	16 April 1975
1–0	v	Cyprus	Limassol	11 May 1975
0–0	v	Northern Ireland	Windsor Park	17 May 1975

This remains the highest number of consecutive games that England have played without conceding a goal.

✦ NAME IN THE BIG RED BOOK ✦

The following is a list of the first five England internationals who were the subject of the television series *This Is Your Life*.

Bobby Charlton	Series 1	Programme 2	26 November 1969
Bobby Moore	Series 2	Programme 33	6 January 1971
Gordon Banks	Series 3	Programme 68	8 March 1972
Jack Charlton	Series 4	Programme 102	2 May 1973
Don Revie	Series 5	Programme 127	24 April 1974

✦ HOME CHAMPIONSHIP RECORD ✦

Rank	Country	P	W	T	L	F	A	Pts
1	*England*	266	161	56	49	661	282	378
2	Scotland	267	141	57	69	574	342	339
3	Wales	266	70	62	134	360	545	202
4	Ireland/N Ireland	265	48	49	168	284	710	145

✦ TROUBLED COMPETITION ✦

The 1980–81 British Championship was left incomplete after both England and Wales refused to travel to Belfast because of the hunger strikes taking place in Northern Ireland's Long Kesh Prison at the time.

[†]*Wales was the first team to score against England under Don Revie's management in a 2–2 draw at Wembley on 21 May 1975.*

⚜
─◦ SIR BOBBY CHARLTON, CBE, OBE ◦─

If you were a child living in the 1960s, apart from Pele, the most famous footballer in the world was Bobby Charlton. Even today the name Bobby Charlton is held in the highest esteem throughout the world, where he is not only remembered for his playing days but as an ambassador for English football.

Bobby Charlton was born on 11 October 1937 in the mining village of Ashington, Northumberland. Bobby's genes dictated that he would be a footballer as his mother, Cissie, was the cousin of Jackie Milburn ("Wor Jackie") the legendary Newcastle United and England centre-forward. In addition, his grandfather and four other uncles were all professional footballers (his uncles George, Jack and Jim played for Leeds United, whilst his uncle Stan played for Leicester City).

On 9 February 1953 the Manchester United scout, Joe Armstrong, watched Bobby Charlton play and speaking of the game Joe said: "I had to peer through a mist, but what I saw was enough. This boy is going to be a world beater." About 18 teams wanted to sign him, but Bobby had committed his future to Matt Busby's Manchester United. On 6 October 1956 he made his Manchester United debut against Charlton Athletic at Old Trafford, scoring twice in a 4–2 victory.

Bobby won everything there was to win in the game; an FA Cup winners' medal, three League Championship winners' medals, a European Cup winners' medal and he was voted European Player of the Year in 1966. Bobby made his international debut against Scotland on 19 April 1958 in Glasgow. England won 4–0 and Charlton scored. In all he played 106 times for England, scoring a record 49 goals, a record that still stands today and he was a member of the 1966 World Cup winning team. Bobby played in four World Cup finals for England (1958, 1962, 1966 and 1970). The great Sir Matt Busby once said of Bobby: "He has broken all records and won everything possible that there is to win. Yet he has remained completely unspoiled."

Whereas George Best possessed the style and Denis Law was flamboyant, Bobby Charlton was a football machine. He had superb skills, tremendous balance and grace, he was athletic and he possessed a cannon of a shot from up to 35 yards out. From the very moment Bobby made his Manchester United debut he was the ultimate professional. In 1973 when Bobby left Old Trafford, he'd made 752 appearances and scored 247 goals in a career that spanned three decades.

⚘ UNBEATEN STREAKS ⚘

England's longest unbeaten streak stands at 20 matches played between the 3–2 home loss to Scotland on 13 April 1889 and the 2–1 away loss to Scotland on 4 April 1896. England's record during this seven-year streak was 16 wins and four draws. In the nineteenth century England only played three times per year, once each against the other home countries, Scotland, Wales and Ireland, in the British Championship. Of the 20 matches, nine were played at home.

The second longest unbeaten streak, and the longest since World War II, involved the 19 matches played between the 3–2 home loss to Austria in a friendly on 20 October 1965 and the 3–2 home British Championship loss to Scotland on 15 April 1967. England's record during this 18-month streak, which also included winning the World Cup, was 16 wins and three draws. Of the 19 matches, 12 were at home.

The third longest unbeaten streak stands at 18 matches played between the 2–1 away loss to Scotland on 7 April 1906 and the 2–0 away loss to Scotland on 2 April 1910. England's record during this four-year streak, which included their first ever games against Continental European opposition (in 1908 and 1909), was 14 wins and four draws. Of these 18 matches, seven were at home.

England also had a 17-match unbeaten streak between the 3–1 loss to the USSR at the 1988 European Championship finals in West Germany on 18 June 1988 and the 2–1 loss to Uruguay in a friendly at Wembley on 22 May 1990. England's record during this 23-month streak was 10 wins and seven draws. Of the 17 games played, 10 were at home.

⚘ BRITISH CHAMPIONSHIP WINNERS ⚘

	Outright Wins	Shared 2-Ways	Shared 3-Ways	Shared 4-Ways	Total Wins
England	34	14	5	1	54
Scotland	24	11	5	1	41
Wales	7	3	1	1	12
Ireland/N Ireland	3	2	2	1	8

⚘ UNDERSTRENGTH WORLD CUP SQUADS ⚘

For the 1954 World Cup finals in Switzerland, England only took 17 of the permitted 22 players. They left five reserves at home. In 1958 and 1962 England only took 20 players instead of the permitted 22.

✠

◦ THE BEST MANAGER WE NEVER HAD ◦

Brian Clough is generally regarded as the best manager never to have managed the national team. As a manager Clough guided both Derby County and Nottingham Forest to the First Division title in 1972 and 1978 respectively, and in 1979 and 1980 his Nottingham Forest side claimed European football's greatest club prize, the European Cup. When Clough was once asked why he thought he never got the England job he said: "They thought I was going to change it lock, stock and barrel. They were shrewd because that's exactly what I would have done."

◦ LITERARY LIONS ◦

In addition to the many former England players who have published their life stories somewhat prosaically under the title *My Autobiography*, here is a selection of recent memoirs from England internationals:

1966 And All that – Sir Geoff Hurst (2001)
Addicted – Tony Adams (1999)
After the Ball – Nobby Stiles (2003)
Farewell But Not Goodbye – Sir Bobby Robson (2005)
Banksy – Gordon Banks (2002)
Biting Talk – Norman Hunter (2004)
Gazza: My Story – Paul Gascoigne (2004)
Greavsie – Jimmy Greaves (2003)
Mr Wright – Ian Wright (1997)
My Side – David Beckham (2003)
My World – David Beckham (2001)
Off The Record – Michael Owen (2004)
Playing Extra Time – Alan Ball (2004)
Priceless – Rodney Marsh (2002)
Psycho – Stuart Pearce (2001)
Right Back To The Beginning – Jimmy Armfield (2004)
Safe Hands – David Seaman (2000)
Super Mac – Malcolm Macdonald (2003)
The Way It Was – Sir Stanley Matthews (2000)
Walking On Water – Brian Clough (2003)

◦ ENGLAND'S REAL MADRID BRIGADE ◦

David Beckham ❖ Laurie Cunningham ❖ Steve McManaman
Michael Owen ❖ Jonathan Woodgate

⟿ ENGLAND'S LAST 10 BAGGIES ⟿

Player	Years
Don Howe	1957–59
Bobby Robson	1957–62
Jeff Astle	1969–70
Tony Brown	1971
Peter Barnes	1979–81
Laurie Cunningham	1979
Bryan Robson	1980–81
Cyrille Regis	1981–82
Derek Statham	1983
Steve Hunt	1984

Did You Know That?
The former England manager, Bobby Robson, the former England trainer, Don Howe, and Derek Kevan, all from WBA, started together in the same England line-up on four occasions. They played against the USSR on 18 May 1958, and in three World Cup finals matches against the USSR, Brazil and Austria in June 1958. A total of 41 West Brom players have been capped by England.

⟿ AULD ENEMIES FINED ⟿

On 16 December 1999, UEFA imposed a fine on the FA for what it considered "improper conduct of the team" during England's 2000 European Championship play-off qualification match against Scotland at Hampden Park on 13 November 1999. Five England players were booked in the game. UEFA also fined Scotland for incurring five cautions during the match. England won 2–0.

⟿ THE YOUNGEST ENGLAND CAPTAINS ⟿

Bobby Moore, 22 years and 48 days.....Czechoslovakia 2 England 4,
29 May 1963

Michael Owen, 22 years and 124 days..............England 4 Paraguay 0,
17 April 2002

Sol Campbell, 23 years and 248 days................Belgium 0 England 0,
24 May 1998

Gerry Francis, 23 years 271 days................Switzerland 1 England 2,
3 September 1975

Billy Wright, 24 years and 245 days...........N Ireland 2 England 6,
9 October 1948

⚜ WORLD CUP FINALS – CHILE 1962 ⚜

The World Cup finals returned to South America in 1962 and were hosted by Chile. England were drawn in a first phase group with Argentina, Bulgaria and Hungary. In their opening game at the finals, England lost 1–2 to the 1958 runners-up, Hungary, on 31 May. Next up for England were Argentina and a 3–1 victory. In their final group game England drew 0–0 with Bulgaria, and progressed to the quarter-finals. On 10 June 1962, England lost their quarter-final game 3–1 to Brazil in Estadio Sausalito, Viña del Mar. Brazil went on to win the World Cup beating Czechoslovakia 3–1 in the final.

FIRST ROUND, GROUP 4

30 MAY 1962, RANCAGUA, 7,938

Hungary (1) 2   v   **England** (0) 1
(Tichy 17, Albert 61)   (Flowers pen 60)

England: Springett, Armfield, Wilson, Moore, Flowers, Norman, Douglas, Greaves, Hitchens, Haynes, Charlton.

---

2 JUNE 1962, RANCAGUA, 9,794

England (2) 3   v   **Argentina** (0) 1
(Flowers pen 17,   (Sanfilippo 81)
Charlton, Greaves 67)

England: Springett, Armfield, Wilson, Moore, Flowers, Norman, Douglas, Greaves, Peacock, Haynes, Charlton.

---

7 JUNE 1962, RANCAGUA, 5,700

England (0) 0   v   **Bulgaria** (0) 0

England: Springett, Armfield, Wilson, Moore, Flowers, Norman, Douglas, Greaves, Peacock, Haynes, Charlton.

Group 4 – Final table

	P	W	D	L	F	A	Pts
Hungary	3	2	1	0	8	2	5
England	3	1	1	1	4	3	3
Argentina	3	1	1	1	2	3	3
Bulgaria	3	0	1	2	1	7	1

QUARTER-FINAL
10 JUNE 1962, VIÑA DEL MAR, 17,736

Brazil (1) 3   **v**   **England** (1) 1
(Garrincha 31, 59, Vava 53)   (Hitchens 38)

England: Springett, Armfield, Wilson, Moore, Flowers,
Norman, Douglas, Greaves, Hitchens,
Haynes, Charlton.

England's 1962 World Cup Finals Squad

1	Ron Springett......(Sheff Wed)	12	Alan Hodgkinson.......(Sheff Utd)
2	Jimmie Armfield......(Blackpool)	13	Derek Kevan*.....................(WBA)
3	Ray Wilson.............(Huddersfield)	14	Stanley Anderson.....(Sunderland)
4	Bobby Robson.....................(WBA)	15	Maurice Norman..................(Spurs)
5	Peter Swan...........(Sheffield Wed)	16	Bobby Moore.............(West Ham)
6	Ron Flowers.....................(Wolves)	17	Bryan Douglas.........(Blackburn)
7	John Connelly..................(Burnley)	18	Roger Hunt...............(Liverpool)
8	Jimmy Greaves.....................(Spurs)	19	Alan Peacock....(Middlesbrough)
9	Gerry Hitchens.......(Inter Milan)	20	George Eastham................(Arsenal)
10	Johnny Haynes.............(Fulham)	21	Don Howe.......................(WBA)
11	Bobby Charlton............(Man Utd)	22	Jimmy Adamson............(Burnley)

Manager: Walter Winterbottom

*On reserve at home.

—⌀ SO NEAR, YET SO FAR ⌀—

England missed out on a place in the Euro 96 Final at Wembley after losing in a penalty shoot-out to Germany in the semi-finals. Here is the tale of the spot kicks:

England		Germany
Shearer scored...............1		Hassler scored
Platt scored....................2		Strunz scored
Pearce scored..................3		Reuter scored
Gascoigne scored.......4		Ziege scored
Sheringham scored....5		Kuntz scored
Southgate missed......6		Möller scored

—⌀ SAMBA KINGS SPOIL EL TEL'S RECORD ⌀—

During his reign as England manager, Terry Venables only tasted defeat once (excluding a penalty shoot-out). Brazil beat England 3–1 at Wembley in 1995.

⚜ ENGLAND XI – ARSENAL ⚜

1
David
SEAMAN

2
Lee
DIXON

6
Martin
KEOWN

5
Tony
ADAMS

3
Nigel
WINTERBURN

7
Ray
PARLOUR

8
Bob
McNAB

4
Paul
MARINER

11
Paul
MERSON

9
Ian
WRIGHT

10
Charlie
GEORGE

Substitutes
Richard **WRIGHT**, Ashley **COLE**, Steve **BOULD**,
David **PLATT**, Cliff **BASTEN**
Manager
Joe **MERCER**

Did You Know That?

Arsenal were founded as Dial Square in 1886 by factory workers at
the Royal Arsenal in Woolwich, London and were then renamed
Royal Arsenal shortly afterwards. In 1891, the club then changed
their name to Woolwich Arsenal after they turned professional
before finally settling on their current name, Arsenal.

⚜ FREAK OWN GOAL ⚜

On 3 June 2000 England played Malta in the National Stadium,
Ta'Qali, in a friendly. In the 31st minute David Carabott missed
a penalty against Richard Wright. The ball hit the post and then
rebounded off Wright and rolled over the goal-line. The goal went
down as a Wright own goal. England won 2–1.

⚜ THE MOST MATCHES AS CAPTAIN ⚜

90 Billy Wright ❖ 90 Bobby Moore

ENGLAND SPELL IT OUT

England players first wore their names on the back of their shirts during the 1992 European Championships in Sweden. England's first game was a 0–0 draw with Denmark in Malmo on 11 June 1992, with the team lining up as follows:

1. Chris Woods............Sheffield Wednesday
2. Keith Curle............Manchester City
3. Stuart Pearce............Nottingham Forest
4. Carlton Palmer............Sheffield Wednesday
5. Des Walker............Nottingham Forest
6. Martin Keown............Everton
7. David Platt............Bari
8. Trevor Steven............Marseille
9. Alan Smith............Arsenal
10. Gary Lineker............Tottenham Hotspur
11. Paul Merson............Arsenal

Tony Daley of Aston Villa replaced Keith Curle, and Neil Webb of Manchester United replaced Paul Merson during the game.

TOP 10 GOALIES

The following is a list of England's Top 10 most capped goalkeepers (up to and including the Denmark game on 17 August 2005):

	Caps
Peter Shilton	125
David Seaman	75
Gordon Banks	73
Ray Clemence	61
Chris Woods	43
Ron Springett	33
David James	33
Henry Hibbs	25
Bert Williams	24
Nigel Martyn & Gil Merrick	23

THE FASTEST GOALS AT WEMBLEY

38 sec, Bryan Robson v Yugoslavia.................... 13 December 1989
44 sec, Bryan Robson v N. Ireland .... 23 February 1982

⚜ ENGLAND'S LAST 10 CHELSEA BLUES ⚜

Player	Years
Tony Dorigo	1989–91
Dennis Wise	1991–2000
Graeme Le Saux	1997–2000
Frank Lampard	2001–present
Joe Cole	2003–present
Wayne Bridge	2003–present
John Terry	2003–present
Glen Johnson	2003–present
Scott Parker	2004
Shaun Wright-Phillips	2005–present

Did You Know That?
Five Chelsea players played against Denmark on 16 November 2003. John Terry and Frank Lampard played the full 90 minutes, Joe Cole started and was substituted after 75 minutes, Glen Johnson came on as a substitute after 15 minutes and Wayne Bridge came on as a second-half substitute. A total of 40 Chelsea players have been capped by England up to the end of 2005.

⚜ THE LIONS ROAR (5) ⚜

"I could see Colin Hendry coming in, so I flicked it over his head and volleyed it. God, the feeling when I scored was magnificent! I'm so glad I scored that goal."
Paul Gascoigne *on his wonder goal against Scotland at Euro 96.*

⚜ ON TARGET AGAINST SCOTLAND ⚜

The last 10 England players to score against Scotland are:

Paul Scholes (2)	Hampden Park	13 November 1999
Paul Gascoigne	Wembley	15 June 1996
Alan Shearer	Wembley	15 June 1996
Steve Bull	Hampden Park	27 May 1989
Chris Waddle	Hampden Park	27 May 1989
Peter Beardsley	Wembley	21 May 1988
Glenn Hoddle	Wembley	23 April 1986
Terry Butcher	Wembley	23 April 1986
Tony Woodcock	Hampden Park	26 May 1984
Gordon Cowans	Wembley	1 June 1983

✠

⟶ EVER PRESENT ⟶

Billy Wright of Wolverhampton Wanderers holds the record for the highest number of consecutive appearances for England, with 70. The run began on 3 October 1951 in the 2–2 draw with France at Arsenal Stadium, and ended in the 8–1 win against the USA at Wrigley Field, Los Angeles, on 28 May 1959, which was also Wright's 105th and last appearance for England. Wright was England's captain in all 70 matches.

⟶ BUSBY BABES ⟶

The following England internationals perished as a result of the Munich Air Disaster on 6 February 1958:

Roger Byrne 33 caps (0 goals) ❖ Duncan Edwards 18 caps (5 goals)
David Pegg 1 cap (0 goals) ❖ Tommy Taylor 19 caps (16 goals)

⟶ WHAT'S IN A NAME? ⟶

Three pairs of England players have shared the same name:

Alan Smith..............(Leeds United, Manchester United 2001–present)
Alan Smith...(Arsenal, 1989–92)
Gary Stevens..............................(Tottenham Hotspur, 1985–86)
Gary Stevens..(Everton, 1985–92)
Dave Watson.........................(Norwich City, Everton, 1984–88)
Dave Watson..............(Sunderland, Manchester City, Werder Bremen,
Southampton, Stoke City, 1974–82)

⟶ THE MAGNIFICENT SEVEN ⟶

David Seaman, whose England career began under Bobby Robson on 16 November 1988, played his 75th and last international under Sven-Goran Eriksson on 16 October 2002. In between David played for England under five other England managers: Graham Taylor, Terry Venables, Glenn Hoddle, caretaker Howard Wilkinson and Kevin Keegan. David might well have played for eight different England managers, but when Peter Taylor took charge of the national team for one match on 15 November 2000, the friendly against Italy, he picked an experimental squad comprised mainly of younger players. David James played in goal and England lost 1–0.

✑ NINE GOALS ON THE TROT ✑

Tinsley Lindley, of Cambridge University, scored in nine consecutive England internationals between 13 March 1886 and 31 March 1888. The goals were spread over a three-year period because in the nineteenth century England only played three matches per season, one each against the other home countries in the British Home International Championships. In his total of 13 internationals for England, Lindley scored 15 times – seven goals against Ireland, five against Wales and three against Scotland.

✑ ENGLAND'S CHAMPIONS OF EUROPE ✑

The following England players have won Champions League medals with their clubs:

David Beckham	Manchester United
Wes Brown	Manchester United
Nicky Butt	Manchester United
Jamie Carragher	Liverpool
Andy Cole	Manchester United
Steven Gerrard	Liverpool
Owen Hargreaves	Bayern Munich
Steve McManaman	Real Madrid
Gary Neville	Manchester United
Phil Neville	Manchester United
Paul Scholes	Manchester United
Teddy Sheringham	Manchester United

✑ THE FASTEST GOAL BY A SUB ✑

10 seconds by Teddy Sheringham v Greece – Old Trafford, 6 October 2001

✑ MOST GOALS SCORED IN A MATCH ✑

England scored 13 goals twice against Ireland. On 18 February 1882 England won 13–0 in Belfast, and on 18 February 1899 England beat Ireland 13–2 in Sunderland. The 13–0 victory is also England's biggest ever margin of victory.[†]

[†] *England have also scored two 10–0 victories: over Portugal in Lisbon on 25 May 1947, and over the USA in New York City on 27 May 1947.*

☖ CAPPED WITHOUT A KICK ☖

At the very moment when Phil Neal of Liverpool came on for Kenny Samson of Arsenal in England's opening game against France during the 1982 World Cup finals in Spain, the referee blew the final whistle. Alan Smith came on as a substitute in injury time against Slovakia in Bratislava in the European Championship preliminary match on 12 October 2002, when the ball was out of play behind England's goal. As soon as David Seaman took the resulting goal-kick, the final whistle blew. Both players earned caps without even touching the ball.

☖ HEAD-TO-HEAD WITH BRAZIL ☖

	Played	Won	Drawn	Lost	For	Against
WC Finals	4	0	1	3	2	6
ECQ Home	0	0	0	0	0	0
ECQ Away	0	0	0	0	0	0
EC Finals	0	0	0	0	0	0
Friendly Home	9	2	5	2	11	11
Friendly Away	8	1	2	5	5	12
Total	21	3	8	10	18	29

☖ END OF THE BATTLE OF BRITAIN ☖

In 1983 England announced that they would no longer play Wales and Northern Ireland as they could not find the time in their crowded calendar. Scotland quickly followed suit, and as a result the 1983–84 British Championship, exactly 100 years after the first, was the last. Northern Ireland won the last ever British Championship, only their third outright success ever in the competition, and kept the trophy.

☖ RECORD MATCH RECEIPTS ☖

£4,100,000 v Germany (Euro 96 semi-final – Wembley, 26 June 1996)

☖ WEMBLEY FOR MONOPOLY MONEY ☖

When Waddington's released their updated version of the famous Monopoly Board Game in 2005, the new Wembley Stadium was one of the properties available for purchase even before it was finished.

∽ WORLD CUP FINALS – ENGLAND 1966 ∾

Between 11 and 30 July 1966, England played host to the 1966 World Cup finals. Prior to the 1966 World Cup finals the Jules Rimet Trophy was stolen from an exhibition display in London. Seven days later a dog named "Pickles" found it wrapped in newspaper under a garden hedge. England played their opening game in front of 75,000 passionate fans at Wembley and drew 0–0 with Uruguay. Next up for England was Mexico at Wembley where goals from Bobby Charlton and Roger Hunt sealed a 2–0 win. England then beat France 2–0, both goals scored by Hunt, to top the group with 5 points.

On 23 July, England met Argentina at Wembley in the quarter-final with 88,000 fans cheering them on. The Argentinians played a cynically dirty game with their captain, Antonio Rattin, being shown the red card. Rattin refused to leave the pitch and pandemonium ensued as he stayed on the field for 10 minutes. England eventually won the game 1–0 thanks to a goal from Geoff Hurst. On 26 July, England faced Portugal at Wembley in the semi-finals, winning a hard fought match 2–1 with Bobby Charlton netting both goals.

England had reached their first World Cup final and West Germany, winners in 1954, awaited them at Wembley on 30 July 1966. No one who witnessed it will ever forget the 1966 World Cup final. Very little separated the two teams on the pitch, with the score at 1–1 at half-time and 2–2 at the end of 90 minutes. Helmut Haller had put the Germans ahead, Hurst equalized, Peters made it 2–1 to England but with just a few minutes of normal time remaining, Wolfgang Weber equalised for the Germans. Extra-time was required for the first time in a World Cup Final.

In the 11th minute of extra-time, Geoff Hurst had a shot from only a few yards out which struck the underside of the crossbar, bounced down, on or just over the line, and was then cleared by the German defence. Swedish referee, Gottfried Dienst, was unsure if the ball had crossed the line and consulted his Russian linesman, Tofik Bakhramov. Bakhramov delighted the vast majority of the Wembley crowd by indicating that the ball had crossed the line. The referee momentously awarded the goal. However, what was not in dispute was Hurst's third, and England's fourth goal. With only a minute of the extra thirty remaining, the West Germans sent everyone except their goalkeeper forward in a frenzied attempt to score a dramatic last-minute equalizer. But England had other ideas. Bobby Moore picked out the unmarked Geoff Hurst with a long pass from defence. Hurst pushed the ball in front of him, then bore down on the West German goal and blasted it into the net. England had won the World Cup.

FIRST ROUND, GROUP 1
11 JULY 1966, WEMBLEY, 75,000
England (0) **0**   v   **Uruguay** (0) **0**

England: Banks, Cohen, Wilson, Charlton J., Moore,
Stiles, Ball, Charlton R., Connelly,
Greaves, Hunt.

---

16 JULY 1966, WEMBLEY, 85,000
England (1) **2**   v   **Mexico** (0) **0**
(Charlton R. 37, Hunt 75)

England: Banks, Cohen, Wilson, Charlton J., Moore,
Stiles, Peters, Charlton R., Paine,
Greaves, Hunt.

---

20 JULY 1966, WEMBLEY, 92,500
England (1) **2**   v   **France** (0) **0**
(Charlton R. 37, Hunt 75)

England: Banks, Cohen, Wilson, Charlton J., Moore,
Stiles, Peters, Charlton R., Paine,
Greaves, Hunt.

Group 1 – Final table

	P	W	D	L	F	A	Pts
England	3	2	1	0	4	0	5
Uruguay	3	1	2	0	2	1	4
Mexico	3	0	2	1	1	3	2
France	3	0	1	2	2	5	1

QUARTER-FINAL
23 JULY 1966, WEMBLEY 88,000
England (0) **1**   v   **Argentina** (0) **0**
(Hurst 78)

England: Banks, Cohen, Wilson, Charlton J., Moore,
Stiles, Peters, Charlton R., Ball,
Hurst, Hunt.

SEMI-FINAL

26 JULY 1966, WEMBLEY 90,000

England (1) 2   **v**   **Portugal** (0) 1

(Charlton R. 30,80)   (Eusebio (pen) 82)

England: Banks, Cohen, Wilson, Charlton J., Moore,
Stiles, Peters, Charlton R., Ball,
Hurst, Hunt.

FINAL

30 JULY 1966, WEMBLEY 93,000

England (1) 4   **v**   **West Germany** (2) 2

(Hurst 18, 101, 120,   (Haller 12, Weber 89)
Peters 78)

England: Banks, Cohen, Wilson, Charlton J., Moore,
Stiles, Peters, Charlton R., Ball,
Hurst, Hunt.

England's 1966 World Cup Finals Squad

1	Gordon Banks *(Leicester City)*	12	Ron Springett *(Sheff Wed)*
2	George Cohen *(Fulham)*	13	Peter Bonetti *(Chelsea)*
3	Ray Wilson *(Everton)*	14	Jimmy Armfield *(Blackpool)*
4	Nobby Stiles *(Man Utd)*	15	Gerry Byrne *(Liverpool)*
5	Jackie Charlton *(Leeds Utd)*	16	Martin Peters *(West Ham)*
6	Bobby Moore *(West Ham)*	17	Ron Flowers *(Wolves)*
7	Alan Ball *(Blackpool)*	18	Norman Hunter *(Leeds Utd)*
8	Jimmy Greaves *(Spurs)*	19	Terry Paine *(Southampton)*
9	Bobby Charlton *(Man Utd)*	20	Ian Callaghan *(Liverpool)*
10	Geoff Hurst *(West Ham)*	21	Roger Hunt *(Liverpool)*
11	John Connelly *(Man Utd)*	22	George Eastham *(Arsenal)*

Manager: Alf Ramsey

Did You Know That?

Antonio Rattin was the first player to be sent off at Wembley in a
senior international football match. Throughout their 1966 World
Cup Finals campaign, England played without wingers using a
4–4–2 formation, becoming dubbed the "Wingless Wonders".

✧ THE OLDEST CAP ✧

Stanley Matthews v Denmark – Copenhagen (42 years and 104 days)
15 May 1957

⟶ BOBBY MOORE, OBE ⟵

Bobby Moore was born Robert Frederick Chelsea Moore on 12 April 1941 in Barking, London. Bobby signed schoolboy forms for the Hammers in August 1956 and, on 2 October 1957, he made his debut for the England Youth Team. In May 1958 he signed as a professional for West Ham United and, four months later, he made his senior debut for the club. Further debuts followed in 1960 (England Under-23s) and in 1961 (FA Cup) before he made the first of his 108 international appearances for England in a match against Peru on 20 May 1962. England won 4–0 in Lima.

On 20 May 1963, Bobby captained England for the first time when they beat Czechoslovakia 4–2 in Bratislava. Bobby later captained England a further 89 times, to share the record with the legendary Billy Wright for having captained England the most times (90). With West Ham things went well for the young central defender. In May 1964 he captained the Hammers to FA Cup success over Preston North End at Wembley, and the same season was named the Football Writers' Player of the Year.

In 1964–65, West Ham United entered the European Cup Winners' Cup, and Bobby played his first European game on 23 September 1964 against Gantoise of Belgium. The following May, Bobby captained the Hammers to European Cup Winners' Cup Final success when they beat 1860 Munich at Wembley. Bobby was now an established player at both club and international level.

On 30 July 1966, Bobby captained England to their greatest ever triumph, the 4–2 extra-time win over West Germany in the World Cup Final at Wembley. He was voted the 1966 BBC Sports Personality of the Year and the 1966 British Sports Writers' Association Sportsman of the Year and in 1967, he was awarded the OBE for his services to the game.

On 14 February 1973, Bobby captained England in his 100th international appearance for his country: England won 5–0 in a friendly at Hampden Park. Three days later, Bobby played his 510th game for West Ham surpassing Jimmy Ruffell's previous record of 509 appearances. On 14 November 1973, he played for, and captained England, for the last time in a 1–0 defeat to Italy at Wembley.

The following March, Bobby joined Fulham and helped them to the 1975 FA Cup Final, where they lost 2–0 to West Ham. He officially retired in 1977 but later played in the North American Soccer League for the Seattle Sounders. Bobby died of cancer on 24 February 1993.

⚜ ENGLAND XI – LEEDS UNITED ⚜

1
Nigel
MARTYN

2   **5**   **6**   **3**
Paul   Jack   Norman   Tony
REANEY *CHARLTON* *HUNTER* *DORIGO*

7   **4**   **8**   **11**
David   Paul   Tony   Mike
BATTY   *MADELEY* *CURRIE* *O'GRADY*

9   **10**
Mick   Allan
JONES   *CLARKE*

Substitutes
Paul *ROBINSON*, Terry *COOPER*, Trevor *CHERRY*,
Rio *FERDINAND*, Alan *SMITH*
Manager
Don *REVIE*

Did You Know That?

Leeds United's predecessor club, Leeds City FC, was formed in 1904 before it was disbanded in 1919 by the Football Association after financial irregularities. From the old club Leeds United AFC was formed and turned professional in 1920 taking the place of Leeds City's reserve side in the Midland League.

⚜ KEEGAN'S BRIEF SOJOURN ⚜

Because of England's disastrous World Cup qualification record during the 1970s, Kevin Keegan only played 26 minutes' football in World Cup Final tournaments. He came on as a substitute in England's last game of the 1982 finals against the host nation, Spain.

⚜ THE MOST PLAYERS FROM ONE CLUB ⚜

7 Arsenal – England v Italy – Highbury, 14 November 1934
7 Man Utd – England v Albania – Tirana, 28 March 2001

⚜

⟶ ENGLAND'S NINE WORLD CUP CAPTAINS ⟵

Only nine players have led England in World Cup finals since they participated in their first finals in 1950. England were led by their first-choice captains Billy Wright in 1950, 1954 and 1958, Johnny Haynes in 1962, and Bobby Moore in 1966 and 1970. England failed to qualify for the 1974 and 1978 finals. Mick Mills was England's stand-in captain for the 1982 finals as a result of Kevin Keegan's injury, although Keegan did travel and play in the 1982 finals. Bryan Robson was the England captain for both the 1986 and 1990 finals but injuries in both tournaments restricted his appearances.

In 1986 in Mexico, a long-standing shoulder injury forced Robson to leave the pitch during the first half of England's second group game against Morocco, and he did not play any further part in the tournament. Ray Wilkins, his Manchester United team-mate, took over the captain's armband in England's next game against Morocco, but after he was sent off in this game he handed the armband to Peter Shilton. Shilton then captained England in their wins over Poland and Paraguay, and in their loss to Argentina in the "Hand of God" game.

Another injury forced Bryan Robson's withdrawal in the second group match against Holland at the 1990 finals in Italy. Terry Butcher and Peter Shilton both filled in as captain. Shilton was captain for two matches in which Butcher did not play: the third group match against Egypt and the third-place play-off game against Italy. Butcher took over the captaincy for the Belgium, Cameroon and Germany games.

At the 1998 finals in France, Alan Shearer captained England in all four of their games, and in 2002 David Beckham was Sven-Goran Eriksson's choice as team leader. Despite going into the 2002 finals with an injury, Beckham captained the England side in each of their five games. However, he was taken off in the 63rd minute of England's opening game with Sweden, with the captain's armband going to Michael Owen. In England's four remaining matches Beckham managed to last the full 90 minutes.

⟶ THE LIONS ROAR (6) ⟵

"I still get excited when I see the save on TV; it's been shown so many times, and of course it's nice when people talk about it being the greatest save ever."
Gordon Banks reflects on his miraculous save from a Pele header in the first- round match against Brazil at the 1970 World Cup finals.

‑✧ ENGLAND'S LAST 10 RED DEVILS ✧‑

Player	Years
Phil Neville	1996–2005
David Beckham	1996–2003
Nicky Butt	1997–2004
Paul Scholes	1997–2004
Teddy Sheringham	1997–2001
Wes Brown	1999–2005
Rio Ferdinand	2002–present
Alan Smith	2004–05
Wayne Rooney	2004–present
Kieran Richardson	2005

Did You Know That?
Six United players were on the pitch against Spain at Villa Park in Sven-Goran Eriksson's first match in charge. Phil Neville, David Beckham, Nicky Butt, Paul Scholes and Andrew Cole all started, with Gary Neville the substitute. A total of 54 Manchester United players have been capped by England.

‑✧ MOST WORLD CUP FINAL TOURNAMENTS ✧‑

Seven England players have appeared in three World Cup finals. Billy Wright and Tom Finney played in the 1950, 1954 and 1958 tournaments. Bobby Charlton and Bobby Moore appeared in the 1962, 1966 and 1970 tournaments. And Peter Shilton, Terry Butcher and Bryan Robson played in the 1982, 1986 and 1990 tournaments.

‑✧ HEAD-TO-HEAD WITH FRANCE ✧‑

	Played	Won	Drawn	Lost	For	Against
WC Finals	2	2	0	0	5	1
ECQ Home	1	0	1	0	1	1
ECQ Away	1	0	0	1	2	5
EC Finals	2	0	1	1	1	2
Friendly Home	7	5	1	1	20	5
Friendly Away	13	9	1	3	36	18
Total	26	16	4	6	65	32

‑✧ RECORD WIN AT WEMBLEY ✧‑

England 9 Luxembourg 0 – Wembley, 15 December 1982

⚜

⎯⟶ RUSH GOALIE ⟵⎯

In England's first ever international, against Scotland in Glasgow on 30 November 1872, W.J. Maynard, a winger with the 1st Surrey Rifles, played in goal for England. In the second half[†] Maynard changed places with Robert Barker, the Hertfordshire Rangers forward, and played up front in his place. Both Maynard and Barker kept clean sheets as the game ended 0–0.

⎯⟶ RECORD ATTENDANCES ⟵⎯

Home

100,000	England v	Austria	Wembley,	28 November 1951
100,000	England v	Hungary	Wembley,	23 November 1953
100,000	England v	West Germany	Wembley,	1 December 1954
100,000	England v	USSR	Wembley,	22 October 1958
100,000	England v	Portugal	Wembley,	25 October 1961
100,000	England v	Rest of World	Wembley,	23 October 1963
100,000	England v	Spain	Wembley,	3 April 1968
100,000	England v	Portugal	Wembley,	10 December 1969
100,000	England v	Northern Ireland	Wembley,	21 April 1970
100,000	England v	West Germany	Wembley,	29 April 1972
100,000	England v	Poland	Wembley,	17 October 1973
100,000	England v	West Germany	Wembley,	12 March 1975
100,000	England v	Scotland	Wembley,	26 May 1979

Away

160,000	Brazil v England	Maracana, Rio, 13 May 1959
149,547	England v Scotland	Hampden Park, 17 April 1937

⎯⟶ UNDEFEATED BUT OUT ⟵⎯

England were put out of the 1982 World Cup finals without losing a single game. Of their five games they won three and drew two. England won Group 4 by winning all three games (against Czechoslovakia, France and Kuwait), and in the next phase of the tournament went into Group B with host nation Spain, and West Germany. England drew 0–0 with West Germany and 0–0 with Spain, and the Germans qualified from the group, having beaten Spain.

[†]*In the first four official England matches there was no half-time break. Teams changed ends after they scored, which meant no change of ends at all in this game. The half-time break as we know it today was not introduced until 1876.*

EUROPEAN CHAMPIONSHIP 1968

England did not participate in the first European Championship which was played in France in 1960, and in 1964 England failed to qualify from the preliminary stages of the competition for the finals in Spain. England's first taste of European Championship finals matches came in Italy in 1968. UEFA allowed the British Home International Championship for the 1966–67 and 1967–68 seasons to serve as the preliminary competition for qualification to the 1968 Championship. England topped the two-season group ahead of Scotland, Wales and Northern Ireland. To qualify for the finals in Italy, England had to beat Spain in a final qualifying game. On 3 April 1968 England beat Spain 1–0 at Wembley thanks to a Bobby Charlton goal, and in the return match in Real Madrid's Estadio Santiago Bernabeu on 8 May 1968, England beat the Spanish 3–1 with goals from Charlton again, Roger Hunt and Martin Peters.

At the Finals, England lost 1–0 to Yugoslavia in Florence, when Alan Mullery became the first England player to be sent off. However, England won the third place play-off match 2–0 against the USSR in Rome with goals from Bobby Charlton and Geoff Hurst.

Italy met Yugoslavia in the Final on 8 June 1968 and the game ended 0–0. In the replay two days later, the host nation beat the Yugoslavs 2–0 in the Stadio Olimpico, Rome, with goals from Luigi Riva and Pietro Anastasi.

SEMI-FINAL

5 JUNE 1968, FLORENCE, 21,800

Yugoslavia (0) 1 v **England** (0) 0
(Dzajic, 86)

England: Banks, Newton, Wilson, Labone, Moore, Ball, Hunter, Mullery, Peters, Hunt, Charlton.

THIRD-PLACE PLAY-OFF

England (1) 2 v **Soviet Union** (0) 0
(Charlton 40, Hurst 63)

England: Banks, Wright, Wilson, Stiles, Labone, Moore, Hunter, Peters, Hunt, Charlton, Hurst.

England's 1968 European Championship Finals Squad

1	Gordon Banks *(Leicester City)*	12	Alex Stepney *(Man Utd)*
2	Keith Newton *(Blackburn)*	13	Gordon West *(Everton)*
3	Ray Wilson *(Everton)*	14	Cyril Knowles *(Spurs)*
4	Alan Mullery *(Spurs)*	15	Jack Charlton *(Leeds Utd)*
5	Brian Labone *(Everton)*	16	Tommy Wright *(Everton)*
6	Bobby Moore *(West Ham)*	17	Nobby Stiles *(Man Utd)*
7	Alan Ball *(Everton)*	18	Mike Summerbee *(Man City)*
8	Roger Hunt *(Liverpool)*	19	Norman Hunter *(Leeds Utd)*
9	Bobby Charlton *(Man Utd)*	20	Colin Bell *(Man City)*
10	Geoff Hurst *(West Ham)*	21	Jimmy Greaves *(Spurs)*
11	Martin Peters *(West Ham)*	22	Peter Thompson *(Liverpool)*

Manager: Sir Alf Ramsey

Did You Know That?

In 1968, UEFA renamed the "European Nations Cup" the "European Football Championship" with 31 teams entering the tournament. Up until 1976, only four teams entered the final tournament but from 1980 eight teams competed and then in 1996, sixteen teams played in the final tournament. Germany has triumphed the most times, with three victories.

⟡ DUAL CAPTAIN OF ENGLAND ⟡

Reginald Erskine "Tip" Foster, is the only man to captain England at cricket and football. He made his international debut for England's football team on 28 March 1900 in a 1–1 draw with Wales in Cardiff in the British Home International Championship. In his second football international, he scored twice in a 3–0 win over Ireland on 9 March 1901; he scored again in a 6–0 win over Wales on 18 March 1901; he played in a 2–2 draw with Scotland on 18 March 1901 and, on 3 March 1902, he captained England in his fifth and last game for his country in a 0–0 draw with Wales. He won his first England cap as a player for Oxford University, and his next four as a member of the Corinthians team. (During the 1880s a large number of Oxford University players and Corinthians represented England at international level.) In December 1903, he marked his debut in Test cricket with an amazing innings, which to this day remains the highest score by a player in his first Test, and is still the highest ever score by an Englishman on Australian soil. Foster scored 287 as England hit a match winning total of 577. He played in eight Tests for England, captaining the side against South Africa in 1907. Foster suffered from diabetes and died in 1914 aged just 36.

⚜ GAZZA'S TEARS ⚜

When Paul Gascoigne was booked in England's World Cup semi-final game against Germany in Stadio Della Alpi in Turin, Italy, on 4 July 1990, he knew he would miss the Final if England got there. When this realization sunk in Gazza burst into tears, leading Gary Lineker to look across to the England bench, and he could clearly be seen mouthing "Have a word with him." Of course England lost to Germany in the penalty shoot-out with Germany going on to beat Argentina in the Final. Paul Gascoigne was capped 57 times by England and scored 10 international goals.

⚜ SIMPLY THE BEST ⚜

The following England internationals won the European Player of the Year Award:

Stanley Matthews......1956.....(Blackpool – inaugural winner)
Bobby Charlton.........1966................(Manchester United)
Kevin Keegan...........1978.......................(SV Hamburg)
Kevin Keegan...........1979.......................(SV Hamburg)

⚜ HONOURS EVEN AT WEMBLEY ⚜

Nations with an equal win/loss or draw ratio with England at Wembley are:

Brazil ✤ Colombia ✤ Croatia ✤ The Rest of Europe ✤ Romania
Saudi Arabia ✤ Sweden ✤ Uruguay

⚜ ONE-KICK INTERNATIONAL ⚜

Jim Barrett holds the unenviable record of having only one kick at the ball in an international for England. He played his only game for England on 22 October 1928 against Northern Ireland in Liverpool, but had to leave the field when he was injured. Ten-man England won 2–1. Jim died, aged 63, on 25 November 1970.

⚜ ENGLAND'S PRESTON MANAGERS ⚜

William Scott (1949–1953) ✤ Clifford Britton (1956–1961)
Bobby Charlton (1973–1975) ✤ Nobby Stiles (1977–1981)
Brian Kidd (1986)

⟿ ENGLAND'S BAND OF BROTHERS ⟿

Twenty sets of brothers have represented England at international level:

J. C. & W. E. Clegg *(Sheffield Wednesday, 1872 & Sheffield Wednesday, Sheffield Albion, 1873–79)*; **C. F. W. & G. H. H. Heron** *(Wanderers, 1876 & Uxbridge, Wanderers, 1873–78)*; **H. E. & W. S. Rawson** *(Royal Engineers, 1875 & Oxford University, 1875–77)*; **A. W. & H. A. Cursham** *(Notts County, 1876–83 & Notts County, 1880–84)*; **A. & E. Lyttelton** *(Cambridge University, 1877 & Cambridge University, 1878)*; **A. L., E. C. & E. H. Bambridge**[†] *(Swifts, 1881–84 & Swifts, 1879–87 & Swifts, 1876)*; **F. W. & J. Hargreaves** *(Blackburn Rovers, 1880–82 & Blackburn Rovers, 1881)*; **A. T. C. & C. F. Dobson** *(Notts County, 1882–84 & Notts County, 1886)*; **C. P. & G. P. Wilson** *(Hendon, 1884 & Corinthians, 1900)*; **A. M. & P. M. Walters** *(Cambridge University, Old Carthusians, 1885–90 & Oxford University, Old Carthusians, 1885–90)*; **A. & C. Shelton** *(Notts County, 1889–92 & Notts Rangers, 1888)*; **C. & T. Perry** *(WBA, 1890–93 & WBA, 1898)*; **A. G. & R. Topham** *(Casuals, 1894 & Wolverhampton Wanderers, Casuals, 1893–94)*; **Frank & F. R. Forman** *(Nottingham Forest, 1898–1903 & Nottingham Forest, 1899)*; **B. O. & R. Corbett** *(Corinthians, 1901 & Old Malvernians, 1903)*; **F. R. & R. Osborne** *(Fulham, Tottenham Hotspur, 1923–26 & Leicester City, 1928)*; **C. & G. T. Stephenson** *(Huddersfield Town, 1924 & Derby County, Sheffield Wednesday, 1928–31)*; **J. W. & S. C. Smith** *(Portsmouth, 1932 & Leicester City, 1936)*; **J. & R. Charlton** *(Leeds Utd, 1965–70 & Man Utd, 1958–70)*; **G. & P. Neville** *(Man Utd, 1995–present & Man Utd, 1996–present)*.

⟿ NOT SO DAFT ⟿

Henry Daft of Notts County won five caps and scored three goals for England between 1889 and 1892. In his final appearance he got both goals in England's 2–0 win over Ireland in Belfast.

⟿ A RED DEFENSIVE WALL ⟿

When England met Wales at Wembley on 19 May 1971 the entire Liverpool defence played – Emlyn Hughes, Chris Lawler, Larry Lloyd and Tommy Smith. England drew 0–0.

[†]*Arthur, Edward and Ernest Bambridge are the only set of three brothers to have played for England. The three never played together in the same England team, but Arthur and Edward did play together on two occasions.*

⌁ BLOODY BUTCHER ⌁

On 6 September 1989 England met Sweden in the Rasunda Stadium, Stockholm, in a World Cup qualifying game. During the first half Terry Butcher, the Ipswich Town and England captain, suffered a cut head, but he was quickly given a head bandage and played on. By the end of the game the bandage was steeped in blood, and his white England shirt had almost turned red with the blood that had been pouring from his wound. The game ended 0–0 and practically guaranteed England's qualification for the 1990 World Cup finals in Italy.

⌁ THE LIONS ROAR (7) ⌁

"Whether you are white, brown, purple or blue, it's the same. When you are fortunate enough to make an England debut at Wembley, it's the greatest feeling in the world."
Viv Anderson, the first black player to be capped by England.

⌁ 49 COUNTRIES AT WEMBLEY ⌁

England played 49 national teams at the old Wembley and two other representative teams, the Rest of Europe and the Rest of the World.

⌁ ENGLAND'S DAY NUMBERED ⌁

On 17 April 1937 the England team took to the pitch with numbers printed on the back of their shirts for the first time. The team that lost 3–1 to Scotland at Hampden Park, Glasgow, lined up as follows:

1.	Vic Woodley	Chelsea
2.	George Male	Arsenal
3.	Sam Barkas	Manchester City
4.	Cliff Britton	Everton
5.	Alf Young	Huddersfield Town
6.	John Bray	Manchester City
7.	Stanley Matthews	Stoke City
8.	Raich Carter	Sunderland
9.	Freddie Steele	Stoke City
10.	Ronnie Starling	Aston Villa
11.	Joe Johnson	Stoke City

England's goal was scored by Freddie Steele.

⚜ ENGLAND'S LAST 10 EAGLES ⚜

Player	Years
John Alderson	1923
John Byrne	1961
Peter Taylor	1976
Kenny Sansom	1979–80
Ian Wright	1991
Geoff Thomas	1991–92
John Salako	1991
Andy Gray	1991
Nigel Martyn	1992–93
Andy Johnson	2005

Did You Know That?
Three Crystal Palace players started for England when they beat New Zealand 2–0 in Auckland during their 1991 Far East tour. Geoff Thomas, Ian Wright and John Salako all played, while Nigel Martyn was an unused substitute. A total of 11 Crystal Palace players have been capped by England.

⚜ WORLD CUP REGULAR ⚜

Goalkeeper Peter Shilton made 17 consecutive appearances in all of England's games during the 1982, 1986 and 1990 tournaments. Bobby Charlton and Bobby Moore made 14 consecutive appearances, starting all the matches in the 1962, 1966 and 1970 tournaments. And Gary Lineker made 12 consecutive appearances, starting all the matches in the 1986 and 1990 tournaments.

⚜ "ANIMALS" JIBE ⚜

Alf Ramsey described the Argentinian team as "animals" following a bad-tempered 0–0 draw between the two sides during the 1966 World Cup Finals which saw the South American team's captain, Antonio Rattin, sent off. When the final whistle blew Alf ran on to the pitch and prevented George Cohen from swapping shirts with Alberto Gonzalez.

⚜ THE OLDEST ENGLAND SCORER ⚜

Stanley Matthews v N. Ireland – Belfast (41 years and 248 days)
6 October 1956

⚜️ ENGLAND XI – WEST HAM UNITED ⚜️

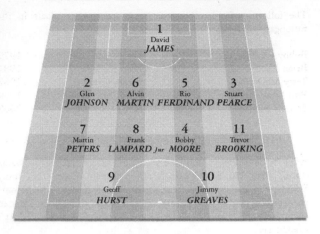

1
David
JAMES

2
Glen
JOHNSON

6
Alvin
MARTIN

5
Rio
FERDINAND

3
Stuart
PEARCE

7
Martin
PETERS

8
Frank
LAMPARD Jnr

4
Bobby
MOORE

11
Trevor
BROOKING

9
Geoff
HURST

10
Jimmy
GREAVES

Substitutes
Paul **KONCHESKY**, Joe **COLE**, Michael **CARRICK**,
Teddy **SHERINGHAM**, Tony **COTTEE**
Manager
Ron **GREENWOOD**

Did You Know That?
The club was founded in 1895 as the works' team from the Thames Ironworks and Shipbuilding Co. Ltd. In 1899, the club joined the Southern League Division Two and in 1900, the club became a limited company and changed its name to West Ham United.

⚜️ ENGLAND'S FIRST EVER GOALSCORER ⚜️

On 8 March 1873, in England's second officially recognized full international, William Stanley-Kenyon of the Wanderers became England's first ever goalscorer in their 4–2 win over Scotland at the Kennington Oval. By scoring twice he also became the first player to score two goals for England in a game.

⚜️ NOT DESTINED TO BE CAPTAIN ⚜️

Kenny Samson played 86 times for England without ever being made captain of the team.

⚜

✒ ON TARGET IN EUROPE ✒

The following England internationals have scored goals in the European Cup Final:

Bobby Charlton (2)	1968	Trevor Francis	1979
Brian Kidd	1968	Alan Kennedy	1981
Terry McDermott	1977	Peter Withe	1982
Phil Neal	1977, 1984	Teddy Sheringham	1999
Tommy Smith	1977	Steven Gerrard	2005

✒ FIRST SUB AT THE WORLD CUP FINALS ✒

After 51 minutes of England's opening game against Romania during the 1970 World Cup finals in Mexico, Everton's Tommy Wright replaced his club team-mate, Keith Newton, to become the first England substitute used at the World Cup finals. Later in the same game, Chelsea's Peter Osgood replaced Manchester City's Francis Lee.

✒ ONE-CAP WONDERS SWAP ROLES ✒

Alan Sunderland (Arsenal) made his international debut for England against Australia in Sydney on 31 May 1980. During the game he was substituted and replaced by Peter Ward (Brighton & Hove Albion) who also won his first cap. Ironically, neither player played for England again.

✒ THE FIRST BLACK ENGLAND CAPTAIN ✒

Ugo Ehiogu for England U21s v Holland – at Portsmouth on 27 April 1993[†]

✒ ODD FEET ✒

On 9 February 1977 Stan Bowles played in England's 2–0 defeat to Holland wearing a Gola boot on his left foot and an Adidas boot on his right foot. Prior to the game Gola offered him £200 to wear their boots in the international, which he accepted. Later the same day Adidas offered him £300 to wear their boots and again he accepted.

[†]*Paul Ince was the first black player to captain England in a full international v USA – at Boston on 9 June 1993*

Mexico hosted the first of its two World Cup finals in 1970. On 2 June 1970 England beat Romania 1–0 in their opening game and then faced the mighty Brazil and lost 1–0 in a game that will forever be remembered for Gordon Banks' unbelievable save from a forceful downward header from the legendary, Pele. Jairzinho scored Brazil's winner and went on to become the first player in World Cup history to score in every game of a finals tournament. England then beat Czechoslovakia 1–0 in their final group game and qualified for the quarter-finals.

On 14 June England played West Germany, in the quarter-final at Estadio Guanajuato, León. Alan Mullery put England ahead in the 31st minute and Martin Peters added a second goal in the 49th minute to give them a 2–0 lead. Franz Beckenbauer then pulled a goal back for West Germany in the 68th minute and two minutes later Sir Alf Ramsey substituted a tiring Bobby Charlton in the hope to keep him fresh for the semi-final. However, Alf's plan backfired on him as Beckenbauer, with Charlton absent, started to exert his own influence on the game. Uwe Seeler equalized for the West Germans in the 76th minute to send the game into extra-time and bring back memories of their extra-time Final encounter at Wembley four years earlier. In the 108th minute Gerd Muller scored West Germany's winner past Peter Bonetti who was deputizing for an ill Gordon Banks in the England goal. West Germany gained their revenge.

FIRST ROUND, GROUP 3

2 JUNE 1970, GUADALAJARA, 50,560

England (0) 1   v   **Romania** (0) 0
(Hurst 65)

England: Banks, Newton (Wright, 51), Cooper, Labone,
Moore, Mullery, Ball, Charlton R., Peters,
Lee (Osgood, 75), Hurst.

---

7 JUNE 1970, GUADALAJARA, 66,843

Romania (0) 1   v   **England** (0) 0
(Jairzinho 59)

England: Banks, Wright, Cooper, Labone,
Moore, Mullery, Ball, Charlton R. (Bell, 63), Peters,
Lee (Astle, 63), Hurst.

✠

11 JUNE 1970, GUADALAJARA, 49,292
England (0) 1   v   Czechoslovakia (2) 2
(Clarke pen 50)

England: Banks, Newton, Cooper, Charlton J.,
Moore, Mullery, Bell, Charlton R. (Ball, 65), Peters,
Clarke, Astle (Osgood, 65).

Group 3 – Final table

	P	W	D	L	F	A	Pts
Brazil	3	3	0	0	8	3	6
England	3	2	0	1	3	1	4
Romania	3	1	0	2	4	5	2
Czechoslovakia	3	0	0	3	2	7	0

QUARTER-FINAL
14 JUNE 1970, LEON, 23,357
West Germany (0) 3   v   England (1) 2
(Beckenbauer 68,   (Mullery 31, Peters 49)
Seeler 76, Müller 108)
England lost after extra time

England: Bonetti, Newton, Cooper, Labone, Moore,
Mullery, Lee, Ball, Charlton R. (Bell, 70), Peters (Hunter, 81),
Hurst, Lee.

England's 1970 World Cup Finals Squad

1	Gordon Banks	*(Stoke City)*	12	Peter Bonetti	*(Chelsea)*
2	Keith Newton	*(Everton)*	13	Alex Stepney	*(Man Utd)*
3	Terry Cooper	*(Leeds Utd)*	14	Tommy Wright	*(Everton)*
4	Alan Mullery	*(Spurs)*	15	Nobby Stiles	*(Man Utd)*
5	Brian Labone	*(Everton)*	16	Emlyn Hughes	*(Liverpool)*
6	Bobby Moore	*(West Ham)*	17	Jackie Charlton	*(Leeds Utd)*
7	Francis Lee	*(Man City)*	18	Norman Hunter	*(Leeds Utd)*
8	Alan Ball	*(Everton)*	19	Colin Bell	*(Man City)*
9	Bobby Charlton	*(Man Utd)*	20	Peter Osgood	*(Chelsea)*
10	Geoff Hurst	*(West Ham)*	21	Allan Clarke	*(Leeds Utd)*
11	Martin Peters	*(Spurs)*	22	Jeff Astle	*(WBA)*

Manager: Sir Alf Ramsey

Did You Know That?
The quarter-final loss to West Germany was Bobby Charlton's 106th
and final game for England. It was also Bonetti's last international.

✠

∽ SIR BOBBY ROBSON, CBE ∽

Bobby began his career at Fulham, making 152 appearances and scoring 68 goals for the Cottagers before moving to West Bromwich Albion in March 1956. During his five years with the Midlands club he was capped by England, scoring twice on his debut against France in November 1957. He played three games at the 1958 World Cup finals in Sweden and went on to win 20 caps. In 1962, after scoring 56 goals in 239 games for the Baggies, he re-signed for Fulham, notching up a further 192 games and nine goals.

On turning to management Bobby had brief spells with Vancouver Whitecaps and Fulham before accepting an offer to manage Ipswich Town. Making good use of the club's youth system, he guided Ipswich to First Division runners-up place in both 1981 and 1982. In 1978 they won the FA Cup for the first and only time in their history and in 1981 Ipswich lifted the UEFA Cup.

In 1982 Bobby left Ipswich to succeed Ron Greenwood as England manager. He led England to two World Cup finals (1986 and 1990), and in 1990 he came close to taking England to the World Cup Final for the first time since 1966. They lost their semi-final to Germany in a dramatic penalty shoot-out.

Bobby then returned to club management at PSV Eindhoven. Having led PSV to the Dutch title twice in a row he took charge of Sporting Lisbon in the summer of 1993, but was controversially sacked in December 1993 when they were top of the Portuguese league after they exited the UEFA Cup. Within months Bobby gained his revenge as his new club FC Porto beat Sporting Lisbon in the Portuguese Cup Final. He then guided FC Porto to the Championship in 1995 and 1996, before moving to Barcelona.

Although Barca won the Spanish Cup and the European Cup Winners' Cup, the championship eluded them and Robson was moved upstairs. In September 1999, after a spell back at PSV, Bobby finally made the long-awaited return to England as manager of Newcastle United. However, early in the 2004–05 season, Sir Bobby was dismissed after failing to win any of their opening four games. "I am massively disappointed not to be able to finish the job I came here to do," he said. "I am black and white through and through and I have had five marvellous years here. I am sorry to leave."

Did You Know That?

When Bobby Robson was the manager of Sporting Lisbon he appointed as his interpreter a young Jose Mourinho. He then kept the future Chelsea manager with him when he moved to FC Porto and Barcelona.

⚜

THE MILLENARY MAN

On 9 September 1987 Neil Webb became the 1,000th player to be capped by England when he came on as a substitute for Glenn Hoddle against West Germany in Dusseldorf. England lost 3–1.

MORTENSEN THE WELSHMAN

England's Stan Mortensen was England's twelfth man for their friendly international with Wales at Wembley in September 1943. When Wales's Ivor Powell was hurt during the game they did not have a reserve to call on, so Mortensen took to the field wearing the Welsh jersey to make the numbers even.

FINDING FAVOUR

Andy Cole won his first four full international caps under four different England managers:

1. 29 March 1995............v Uruguay............................Terry Venables
2. 4 June 1997 ....v Italy..................................Glenn Hoddle
3. 10 February 1999..........v France ....Howard Wilkinson
4. 27 March 1999.............v Poland..............................Kevin Keegan

ROONEY BY NUMBERS

In Wayne Rooney's first four appearances for England he wore a different shirt number each time:

No. 23 as a substitute against Australia on 12 February 2003
No. 18 as a substitute against Liechtenstein on 29 March 2003
No. 9 as a starter against Turkey on 2 April 2003
No. 21 as a substitute against Serbia & Montenegro on 3 June 2003

ENGLAND'S LAST DEFEAT AT WEMBLEY

The 1–0 defeat to Germany in a 2002 World Cup qualifying game on 7 October 2000 marked the end of Wembley Stadium. It was also England's 30th defeat at Wembley over the 76 years the stadium served as their primary home ground.[†]

'Scotland won the most matches against England at Wembley (9), followed by five countries with 2 wins each, Brazil, Italy, Northern Ireland, Germany and West Germany.

⚓ ENGLAND MANAGER FOR ONE GAME ⚓

Peter Taylor was the caretaker manager for one England international. He was in charge for the friendly against Italy in Turin on 15 November 2001, a game England lost 1–0. Taylor gave David Beckham the captain's armband for this game, while Seth Johnson of Derby County became the only player to be given his England debut by Taylor (the 1,102nd player to be capped by England). The team that night for England's 775th game was:

1. David James
2. Gary Neville
3. Rio Ferdinand
4. Gareth Southgate
5. Gareth Barry *(Seth Johnson)*
6. Ray Parlour *(Darren Anderton)*
7. David Beckham
8. Nicky Butt *(Jamie Carragher)*
9. Kieron Dyer *(Robbie Fowler)*
10. Emile Heskey *(Kevin Phillips)*
11. Nicky Barmby

⚓ ENGLAND'S IRISHMAN ⚓

John "Jack" Reynolds was born in Blackburn on 21 February 1869, but when he was a young boy his family moved to Ireland. Before it was discovered that Reynolds was English, he made five appearances for Ireland. Then, on 2 April 1892, he made his England debut in a 4–1 win over Scotland at Hampden Park. Between 1892 and 1897, he made eight appearances at half-back for England while playing for West Bromwich Albion and Aston Villa, including the 2–2 draw with Ireland on 1 March 1894.

Reynolds is the only player to score both for and against England. He scored for Ireland in their 9–1 defeat in Belfast on 15 March 1890, the only international in which he played as a winger. He also scored for England in the 6–0 victory against Wales in 1893, the 5–2 win against Scotland in 1893 and the 2–2 draw with Scotland in 1894, but he failed to score in his only game against Ireland.

⚓ BASTARD CAPPED BY ENGLAND ⚓

Segal Bastard won his one and only international cap in England's 5–4 defeat by Scotland on 18 March 1880.

✂ THE LIONS ROAR (8) ✂

"Neil Webb threw me a towel because I was sobbing my heart out. I had it over my head like a convicted criminal leaving a courthouse."
Stuart Pearce on his reaction to England's penalty shoot-out defeat by Germany in the 1990 World Cup finals.

✂ FAREWELL GOALS AT WEMBLEY ✂

Tony Adams (Arsenal) was the last England player to score at Wembley when England beat the Ukraine in a 2–0 win on 31 May 2000.

Dietmar Hamann was the last player to score an international goal at Wembley when he scored for Germany in their 1–0 win over England on 7 October 2000. It was the last ever international to be played at Wembley and, coincidentally, was Tony Adams's last game for his country.

✂ PASS THE ARMBAND ✂

Three different players captained England in their 0–0 draw with Morocco in Monterrey during the 1986 World Cup finals in Mexico. Bryan Robson dislocated his shoulder and went off injured, passing the captain's armband to his former club-mate, Ray Wilkins. Ten minutes later Wilkins was sent off for throwing the ball at the referee and he handed the armband to Peter Shilton.

✂ EX-PAT ENGLAND CAPTAINS ✂

Up to the end of the 2004–05 season, six players have captained England whilst playing for a foreign club:

David Beckham (Real Madrid) ✷ Paul Ince (Inter Milan)
Kevin Keegan (Hamburg) ✷ David Platt (Juventus/Sampdoria)
Michael Owen (Real Madrid) ✷ Ray Wilkins (AC Milan)

✂ CRAZY HORSE RIDES AGAIN ✂

Emlyn Hughes, known as 'Crazy Horse', was the only player to be capped at full international level by England during the 1960s, 1970s and 1980s:

First game,   5 November 1969 v Holland.........England won 1–0
Last game,   26 March   1980 v Spain.............England won 2–0

⚓ ENGLAND'S LAST 10 BORO BOYS ⚓

Player	Years
David Armstrong	1980
Gary Pallister	1988–89
Nicky Barmby	1995–96
Paul Gascoigne	1997–98
Paul Merson	1998
Paul Ince	1999–2000
Ugo Ehiogu	2001–02
Gareth Southgate	2001–04
Danny Mills (on loan from Leeds United)	2004
Stewart Downing	2005

Did You Know That?
Brian Clough and Ed Holliday played together twice in the same
England team. They both made their England debuts against Wales
on 17 October 1959 in a 1–1 draw in Cardiff (Jimmy Greaves
scored for England). They also started together 11 days later against
Sweden in a 3–2 defeat at Wembley on 28 October 1959. A total of
29 Middlesbrough players have been capped by England.

⚓ COLOUR BAR ⚓

Jack Leslie was a prolific goalscorer for Plymouth Argyle from 1920
to 1935, scoring over 400 goals for his club. Recognizing Leslie's
prowess in front of goal the England selectors picked him to play for
England. However, he then received a note cancelling his call-up to
the England team and stating that the selectors did not realize that
he was "a man of colour". Jack Leslie later remarked in 1982 to Brian
Woolnough: "They must have forgotten I was a coloured boy."

⚓ MOST GOALS IN A SEASON ⚓

The most goals scored by a player in a season for England:

Jimmy Greaves (13) – 1960–61

⚓ PARTNERSHIP DOUBLE ⚓

Tony Adams and Stuart Pearce played alongside Glenn Hoddle in
the England team, and played under Glenn for England when he
became manager.

⟜ THE FIRST BLACK GOALSCORER ⟞

Luther Blissett became the first black player to score for England when he found the net against Luxembourg at Wembley on 15 December 1982. Blissett scored a hat-trick in the game, thereby also becoming the first black player to score a hat-trick for England in a full international.

⟜ LEADERS OF MEN ⟞

During the game between England and Serbia & Montenegro at Leicester City's Walker Stadium on 3 June 2003, four different players captained the England team: Michael Owen, Emile Heskey, Phil Neville and Jamie Carragher. England won 2–1.

⟜ THE MORE THE MERRIER ⟞

England have twice fielded two teams in the same international. England used 11 substitutes against Australia at West Ham United's Boleyn Ground on 12 February 2003, a game they lost 3–1. And then on 5 June 2004 England used another 11 substitutes in the 6–1 friendly win over Iceland at the City of Manchester Stadium.

⟜ HARGREAVES ALL ON HIS OWN ⟞

Owen Hargreaves (Bayern Munich) is the only player to win a full international cap for England without ever having played for an English League club.

⟜ THE FIRST WEMBLEY DEFEAT ⟞

Scotland were the first country to beat England at Wembley. They won 5–1 on 31 March 1928.

⟜ LOWEST ATTENDANCES ⟞

Home
15,628   England v Chile.................................Wembley, 23 May 1989[†]

Away
2,378 England v San Marino..................Bologna, 17 November 1993

[†]*Affected by a tube strike.*

⟶ EUROPEAN CHAMPIONSHIP 1980 ⟵

Having failed to qualify for the final stages of the 1972 and 1976 tournaments, England participated in their second European Championship finals in Italy in 1980. At the finals, England were drawn in Group 2 with Belgium, Spain and the hosts. England drew their opening game 1–1 with Belgium in the Stadio Communale, Turin, lost their next game 1–0 to Italy in the same Stadium and beat the Spanish 2–1 in Stadio San Paolo, Naples. However, it was Belgium who topped the group ahead of Italy, with England finishing in third place and Spain last.

In the Final, Belgium faced West Germany. The Germans dominated the early exchanges and opened the scoring through Horst Hrubesch, who hit an unstoppable shot past Jean-Maire Pfaff. Late on in the game René van de Eycken equalized for the Belgians from the penalty spot, but just as extra-time loomed, Hrubesch scored again to give West Germany a 2–1 victory.

FIRST ROUND, GROUP 2
12 JUNE 1980, TURIN, 15,186

England (1) 1   v   **Belgium** (1) 1
(Wilkins 26)   (Ceulemans 30)

England: Clemence, Neal, Sansom, Watson, Thompson, Coppell (McDermott, 81), Wilkins, Brooking, Keegan, Johnson (Kennedy, 70), Woodcock.

---

15 JUNE 1980, TURIN, 59,649

Italy (0) 1   v   **England** (0) 0
(Tardelli 79)

England: Shilton, Neal, Sansom, Watson, Thompson, Coppell, Wilkins, Kennedy, Keegan, Birtles (Mariner, 76), Woodcock.

---

18 JUNE 1980, NAPLES, 14,440

England (1) 2   v   **Spain** (0) 1
(Brooking 19,   (Dani pen 48)
Woodcock 61)

England: Clemence, Anderson (Cherry, 83), Mills, Watson, Thompson, Wilkins, Hoddle (Mariner, 76), Brooking, McDermott, Keegan, Woodcock.

Group 2 – Final table

	P	W	D	L	F	A	Pts
Belgium	3	1	2	0	3	2	4
Italy	3	1	2	0	1	0	3
England	3	1	1	1	3	3	3
Spain	3	0	1	2	2	4	1

England's 1980 European Championship Finals Squad

1   Ray Clemence.....................*(Liverpool)*
2   Phil Neal............................*(Liverpool)*
3   Kenny Sansom ..... *(Crystal Palace)*
4   Phil Thompson................*(Liverpool)*
5   Dave Watson.............*(Southampton)*
6   Ray Wilkins.....................*(Man Utd)*
7   Kevin Keegan.........*(Hamburg SV)*
8   Steve Coppell ....*(Man Utd)*
9   David Johnson ....*(Liverpool)*
10 Trevor Brooking.........*(West Ham)*
11 Tony Woodcock................*(Arsenal)*
12 Viv Anderson ....*(Notts Forest)*
13 Peter Shilton..............*(Notts Forest)*
14 Trevor Cherry..................*(Leeds Utd)*
15 Emlyn Hughes......................*(Wolves)*
16 Mick Mills................*(Ipswich Town)*
17 Terry McDermott.........*(Liverpool)*
18 Ray Kennedy.....................*(Liverpool)*
19 Glenn Hoddle.......................*(Spurs)*
20 Paul Mariner..........*(Ipswich Town)*
21 Garry Birtles...............*(Notts Forest)*
22 Joe Corrigan....................*(Man City)*

Manager: Ron Greenwood

⟶ ENGLAND'S WELSHMAN ⟵

John Hawley Edwards was born in Shrewsbury in 1850 and made one appearance for England while playing for Shropshire Wanderers, against Scotland in a 2–1 defeat on 7 March 1874 at Hampden Park. In 1876, when he was a player with the Wanderers, he played for Wales in their first international match, also against Scotland. The latter was his only Wales appearance.

⟶ YOUNGEST AND OLDEST GOALKEEPER ⟵

Peter Shilton is England's youngest and oldest goalkeeper. He was 21 years old when he made his debut against East Germany on 21 November 1970. Peter was 40 when he made his last appearance for England on 4 July 1990 against Germany in their 1–1 World Cup semi-final draw in Turin, Italy.

⟶ ENGLAND'S LAST AMATEUR ⟵

The last amateur player to win a full international cap for England was Bernard Joy, who played for the Casuals. England lost the game 3–2 to Belgium in Brussels on 9 May 1936.

ENGLAND XI – TOTTENHAM HOTSPUR

1
Ray
CLEMENCE

2
Alf
RAMSEY

6
Sol
CAMPBELL

5
Gary
MABBUTT

3
Cyril
KNOWLES

7
Chris
WADDLE

8
Glenn
HODDLE

4
Alan
MULLERY

11
Paul
GASCOIGNE

9
Jimmy
GREAVES

10
Gary
LINEKER

Substitutes
Ian *WALKER*, Ledley *KING*, Steve *PERRYMAN*,
Martin *CHIVERS*, Teddy *SHERINGHAM*
Manager
Terry *VENABLES*

Did You Know That?

Tottenham Hotspur are one of only three teams in the 20th century to have won the FA Cup in consecutive years and the only side to have done so on two occasions. Spurs are the only non-league team to have won the FA Cup (1901) and the first British club to win a European trophy (1963).

DRAGON SLAYED

On 16 March 1896, England recorded their biggest ever win over the Welsh, beating them 9–1 in Cardiff (scorers: Bloomer 5, Smith 2, Goodall, Bassett).

FIRST MANAGERIAL SACKING

Despite winning the World Cup, Sir Alf Ramsey was the first England manager to be sacked. His predecessor, Walter Winterbottom, resigned from the post.

⚜

⌐ ON TARGET AGAINST N. IRELAND ⌐

The last 10 England players to get on the score sheet against Northern Ireland are:

Frank Lampard Jnr	Old Trafford	26 March 2005
Michael Owen	Old Trafford	26 March 2005
Joe Cole	Old Trafford	26 March 2005
Chris Waddle	Windsor Park	1 April 1987
Bryan Robson	Windsor Park	1 April 1987
Chris Waddle	Wembley	15 October 1986
Gary Lineker	Wembley	15 October 1986
Mark Hateley	Windsor Park	27 February 1985
Tony Woodcock	Wembley	4 April 1984
Ray Wilkins	Wembley	23 February 1982

⌐ WALES'S ENGLISH BOBBY ⌐

Robert "Bobby" Ernest Evans was born in Chester on 21 November 1885 of Welsh parents. Between 1906 and 1910 (while playing for Wrexham, Aston Villa and Sheffield United) he made 10 international appearances for Wales. He played four times against England, in the 1–0 loss in 1906, the 1–1 draw in 1907, the 7–1 loss in 1908 and the 1–0 loss in 1910. After he scored his only two goals for Wales against Ireland in his tenth and final international match for Wales, the England selectors discovered that he was in fact born in England. He then made four appearances for England, all when he was a Sheffield United player, in 1911 and 1912, including 3–0 and 2–0 victories against Wales. He scored his only England goal on his debut against Ireland in a 2–1 win in Derby on 11 January 1911.

⌐ BACH PLAYS THE RIGHT TUNE ⌐

Philip Bach (Sunderland) won his only cap for England in their 13–2 win over Ireland in Sunderland on 18 February 1899.

⌐ GOAL SHY ⌐

Four players have made in excess of 50 appearances for England without scoring:

Ray Wilson ❖ Des Walker ❖ Gary Neville ❖ Phil Neville

⚜

⚘ ENGLAND'S LAST 10 GUNNERS ⚘

Player	Years
Paul Merson	1991–97
Ian Wright	1992–98
Martin Keown	1993–2002
Steve Bould	1994
David Platt	1995–96
Ray Parlour	1999–2000
Ashley Cole	2001–present
Richard Wright	2001
Sol Campbell	2001–present
Francis Jeffers	2003

Did You Know That?

Arsenal still hold the record for having the highest number of players from the same club starting a game for England. Seven Arsenal players played in the famous "Battle of Highbury" game against the world champions Italy at Arsenal Stadium on 14 November 1934. England won the "friendly" 3–2. Five Arsenal players were originally selected: Frank Moss in goal, captain Eddie Hapgood at left-back, Wilf Copping at left half-back, Ray Bowden at inside-right and Cliff "Boy" Bastin at inside-left. However, when original choices Tom "Snowy" Cooper, the Derby County right-back, and Fred Tilson, the Manchester City centre-forward, were injured on the Saturday before the Italy game, a sixth Arsenal player, right-back George Male, and Tottenham Hotspur forward George Hunt were selected to replace them. However, Hunt then had to withdraw from the team and the selectors chose a seventh Arsenal player, centre-forward Ted Drake, to replace him. A total of 56 Arsenal players have been capped by England up to the end of 2005.

⚘ THE LIONS ROAR (9) ⚘

"I'm just saying to your colleague, the referee's got me the sack. Thank him ever so much for that, won't you."
Graham Taylor *remonstrates with a FIFA official and a linesman during England's doomed World Cup qualifier against Holland in 1993.*

⚘ A WALK IN THE BLACK FOREST ⚘

When England qualified for the 2006 they booked themselves into the luxury Schlosshotel Buhlerhohe in the Black Forest near the popular spa town of Baden-Baden in Germany.

⚜

⤐ THE OLDEST DEBUTANT ⟞

Leslie Compton 38 years and two months v Wales – Roker Park, 15 November 1950

⤐ FOUR-WAY SPLIT ⟞

Season 1955–56 was the only occasion on which all four countries obtained three points each, and the British Home International Championship trophy was shared four ways.

⤐ YOU ONLY PLAY ONCE ⟞

Up to the end of the 2004–05 season England have played eight different countries only once in an international. They are, in alphabetical order: Azerbaijan, Bohemia, Canada, China, Ecuador, Kuwait, Malaysia and South Korea.

⤐ HAT-TRICK HEROES AGAINST THE SCOTS ⟞

Only two players have scored a hat-trick against Scotland in a full international for England:

Dennis Wilshaw......scored 4................Wembley, 2 April 1955 7–2
Jimmy Greaves........scored 3................Wembley, 15 April 1961...9–3

⤐ DUAL INTERNATIONALISTS ⟞

Denis Compton and Willie Watson both represented England at international level in cricket and football.

⤐ KIWI KEN ⟞

Kenneth Armstrong was born in Bradford on 3 June 1924 and made one appearance for England, at right-half in the 7–2 victory against Scotland at Wembley on 2 April 1955. In May 1957 Ken emigrated to New Zealand after making a record 362 League appearances for Chelsea (later broken by Peter Bonetti and then again by Ron Harris). He then made 13 appearances for New Zealand's national side between 1958 and 1964, and became chief coach for the New Zealand Football Association.[†]

Since the early 1960s FIFA has prohibited players from appearing for more than one country.

⟀ BILLY WRIGHT, CBE ⟀

William Ambrose Wright was born won 6 February 1924 in Ironbridge, Shropshire, England. As a boy he supported Arsenal, but when he heard that Wolverhampton Wanderers were advertising in the local newspaper for young boys to attend trials, he made his way aged 14 to Molineux to try his luck. He signed on as a member of the ground staff team in July 1938. Still only 14, he made his debut for Wolves in a B Team game against Walsall Wood in the Walsall Minor League. When he first arrived at the club, the Wolves' manager, Major Frank Buckley, wasn't convinced of Billy's football ability and told him that he did not think that he would make it as a professional footballer. In 1939, shortly after the outbreak of war, Billy made his Wolves debut in a 2–1 victory at Notts County and shortly after the end of World War II, Billy was made the captain of Wolves.

Billy led Wolves to FA Cup glory in 1948–49, and the First Division Championship in 1953–54, 1957–58 and 1958–59. On 28 September 1946, Billy won his first international cap for England in a 7–2 win over Northern Ireland at Windsor Park, Belfast, a game that also witnessed the debut of Tom Finney.

After he made his debut for England in 1946, Billy graced the Three Lions shirt for a further 13 years (missing only three games) and during that time, he won 105 caps and scored three times. England won 60 of the games, drew 23 and lost 21 with one game abandoned. Billy played his last game for England in their 8–1 win over the USA in Los Angeles on 28 May 1959. His record of captaining England 90 times was later equalled by Bobby Moore, while his record 105 caps stood for 20 years until it was broken by Bobby Charlton in 1970.

Billy Wright, captain of Wolves and England, was a one-club man throughout his career, and one of football's greatest ambassadors. In the 541 games he played for Wolves and the 105 times he pulled on an England shirt, he was never cautioned. In 1952 he was voted the Footballer of the Year and played his last league game for Wolves in the penultimate match of their 1958–59 Championship winning season, a 3–0 win over Leicester City at Molineux. He was awarded the CBE in 1959 and retired before the start of the 1959–60 season. Billy said farewell to his adoring fans in their annual pre-season "Colours v Whites" game at Molineux. On 3 September 1994, Billy passed away after a fight against cancer. Today a statue of Billy stands as proud as the man himself outside his beloved Molineux.

~◦ ENGLAND HONOURS LIST ◦~

Knighthoods

John Charles Clegg	1927	Tom Finney	1998
Stanley Matthews	1965	Geoff Hurst	1998
Alf Ramsey	1967	Bobby Robson	2002
Walter Winterbottom	1978	Trevor Brooking	2004
Bobby Charlton	1994		

Commanders of the Order of the British Empire (CBE)

Stanley Matthews	1957	Ron Greenwood	1983
Billy Wright	1959	Bobby Robson	1990
Walter Winterbottom	1972	Tom Finney	1992
Bobby Charlton	1974	Trevor Brooking	1999

Officers of the Order of the British Empire (OBE)

Tom Finney	1961	Kevin Keegan	1982
Walter Winterbottom	1963	Bryan Robson	1990
Bobby Moore	1967	Peter Shilton	1991
Bobby Charlton	1969	Brian Clough	1991
Don Revie	1970	Gary Lineker	1992
Gordon Banks	1970	Nat Lofthouse	1994
Jack Charlton	1974	Jimmy Armfield	2000
Bill Nicholson	1975	Alan Shearer	2001
George Eastham	1975	Graham Taylor	2002
Joe Mercer	1976	David Beckham	2003
Emlyn Hughes	1980		

Members of the Order of the British Empire (MBE)

Norman Creek	1943	Gary Mabbutt	1994
Jimmy Dickinson	1964	John Barnes	1998
Ian Callaghan	1974	Stuart Pearce	1999
Martin Peters	1978	Tony Adams	1999
Geoff Hurst	1979	Viv Anderson	2000
Trevor Brooking	1981	Alan Ball	2000
Alan Mullery	1975	Steve Bull	2000
Terry Paine	1977	George Cohen	2000
Tommy Smith	1977	Roger Hunt	2000
Ray Clemence	1981	Nobby Stiles	2000
Mick Mills	1984	Ray Wilson	2000
Steve Perryman	1984	Ian Wright	2000
Peter Shilton	1986	Colin Bell	2005
Ray Wilkins	1993	Les Ferdinand	2005

⎯ WORLD CUP FINALS – SPAIN 1982 ⎯

At the 1982 World Cup finals, hosted by Spain, England were drawn in Group D in the first round with Czechoslovakia, France and Kuwait. England's first game was on 16 June 1982, a 3–1 win over France. England followed this up with a 2–0 win over Czechoslovakia and a 1–0 win over Kuwait. All of England's Group D games were played in Estadio San Mamés, Bilbao, and they progressed to the second final group stages after topping Group D with maximum points.

England now found themselves in the same group as the host nation, Spain, and old rivals West Germany. Despite not losing a single game at the 1982 finals, England still failed to qualify for the quarter-finals after two goalless draws saw them finish group runners-up to West Germany.

West Germany made it all the way to the Final, where they lost 3–1 to Italy. Rossi, Tardelli and Altobelli scored for the Italians, with Brietner getting a late consolation goal for the Germans.

FIRST ROUND, GROUP 4

BILBAO, 16 JUNE 1982, 44,172

England (1) 3   v   **France** (1) 1
(Robson 1, 67, Mariner 83)   (Soler 24)

England: Shilton, Mills, Sansom (Neal, 90), Thompson, Butcher, Coppell, Robson, Wilkins, Rix, Mariner, Francis.

BILBAO, 20 JUNE 1982, 41,123

England (0) 2   v   **Czechoslovakia** (0) 0
(Francis 62,
(Barmos o.g.) 66)

England: Shilton, Mills, Butcher, Thompson, Butcher, Coppell, Robson (Hoddle, 46), Wilkins, Rix, Mariner, Francis.

BILBAO, 25 JUNE 1982, 39,700

England (1) 1   vs   **Kuwait** (0) 0
(Francis 27)

England: Shilton, Neal, Mills, Thompson, Foster, Coppell, Wilkins, Hoddle, Rix, Mariner, Francis.

Group 4 – Final table

	P	W	D	L	F	A	Pts
England	3	3	0	0	6	1	6
France	3	1	1	1	6	5	3
Czechoslovakia	3	0	2	1	2	4	2
Kuwait	3	0	1	2	2	6	1

SECOND ROUND, GROUP 2

29 JUNE 1982, MADRID, 75,000

West Germany (0) **0**   v   **England** (0) **0**

England: Shilton, Mills, Sansom, Thompson, Butcher,
Coppell, Robson, Wilkins, Rix,
Mariner, Francis (Woodcock, 77).

---

5 JULY 1982, MADRID, 75,000

Spain (0) **0**   v   **England** (0) **0**

England: Shilton, Mills, Sansom, Thompson, Butcher,
Robson, Wilkins, Rix (Brooking, 65), Woodcock (Keegan, 64),
Mariner, Francis.

Group 2 – Final table

	P	W	D	L	F	A	Pts
West Germany	2	1	1	0	2	1	3
England	2	0	2	0	0	0	2
Spain	2	0	1	1	1	2	1

England's 1982 World Cup Finals Squad

1	Ray Clemence .... (*Spurs*)	12	Mick Mills ....(*Ipswich Town*)
2	Viv Anderson ....(*Nottm Forest*)	13	Joe Corrigan ....(*Man City*)
3	Trevor Brooking ......,(*West Ham*)	14	Phil Neal....................(*Liverpool*)
4	Terry Butcher ....(*Ipswich Town*)	15	Graham Rix ....(*Arsenal*)
5	Steve Coppell ....(*Man Utd*)	16	Bryan Robson............(*Man Utd*)
6	Steve Foster ....(*Brighton & H.A.*)	17	Kenny Sansom ....(*Arsenal*)
7	Kevin Keegan ....(*Southampton*)	18	Phil Thompson ....(*Liverpool*)
8	Trevor Francis............(*Man City*)	19	Ray Wilkins..............(*Man Utd*)
9	Glenn Hoddle .... (*Spurs*)	20	Peter Withe.............(*Aston Villa*)
10	Terry McDermott....... (*Liverpool*)	21	Tony Woodcock ....(*Arsenal*)
11	Paul Mariner ....(*Ipswich Town*)	22	Peter Shilton ....(*Nottm Forest*)

Manager: Ron Greenwood

⚜

⚔ ENGLAND'S LAST 10 RAMS ⚖

Player	Years
Bert Mozley	1949
John Lee	1950
Roy McFarland	1971–76
Colin Todd	1972–77
David Nish	1973–74
Kevin Hector	1973
Charlie George	1977
Peter Shilton	1987–90
Mark Wright	1988–91
Seth Johnson	2001

Did You Know That?
Three Derby County players, George Kinsey, Stephen Bloomer and John Goodall, were in the England side that beat Wales 9–1 in Cardiff on 16 March 1896. Bloomer scored five times and Goodall once. A total of 38 Derby County players have been capped by England.

⚔ HODDLE SACKED ⚖

In early 1999 the FA sacked England coach Glenn Hoddle[†] after a routine interview with *The Times* turned out to be a major news story. Hoddle, a committed Christian, suggested that disabled people were being punished for sins in an earlier life. There was an immediate public outcry, and though Hoddle did his best to play it down, the media and political pressure on the FA was huge. In fact the FA were already angered by his dressing-room revelations. After the 1998 World Cup finals, Hoddle had criticised some of the England players in his book *Glenn Hoddle: My World Cup Diary*. The FA had no choice but to release him from his position as national team manager.

⚔ THE NEW GENERATION ⚖

Tony Adams was the first player to play for England who was born after England won the World Cup in 1966. Tony was born on 10 October 1966 and made his England debut against Spain on 18 February 1987.

[†] *The popular Arsenal goalkeeper, Bob Wilson, once remarked of Glenn: "I hear Glenn Hoddle has found God. That must have been one hell of a pass." Glenn made 53 appearances, scoring eight goals, for England between 22 November 1979 (England 2 Bulgaria 0) and 18 June 1988 (England 1 USSR 3).*

⚜

⚘ ENGLAND PLAYER REJECTS WALES ⚘

Robert Topham of Wolverhampton Wanderers, who played for England as a winger and inside-forward in the 6–1 victory against Ireland in Birmingham on 25 February 1893 and the 5–1 win against Wales in 1894, was selected to play for Wales against Scotland in 1885, but did not accept the invitation.

⚘ VETERANS OF '66 ⚘

In 1981 England played West Germany in a charity match marking the fifteenth anniversary of the 1966 World Cup Final when England beat West Germany 4–2 at Wembley. Most of the players were now in their forties. Franz Beckenbauer put the Germans ahead early in the second half and Wolfgang Overath made it 2–0. However, Bobby Moore scored England's first goal before Bobby Charlton saved England's blushes with a goal seven minutes from time to earn England's 1966 World Cup winning team a 2–2 draw. Of the original team only George Cohen and Ray Wilson missed the game.

⚘ ENGLAND'S MAN CITY MANAGERS ⚘

Joe Mercer (July 1965 to June 1972)
Peter Reid (November 1990 to August 1993)
Alan Ball (June 1995 to August 1996)
Steve Coppell (October 1996 to November 1996)
Phil Neal (caretaker – November 1996 to December 1996)
Joe Royle (February 1998 to June 2001)
Kevin Keegan (June 2001 to May 2005)
Stuart Pearce (June 2005 – present)

⚘ ENGLAND'S FIRST EVER CAPTAIN ⚘

Cuthbert Ottaway of Oxford University captained England in their first recognized full international in a match against Scotland, in Glasgow, on 30 November 1872. The game ended 0–0.

⚘ COLLECTORS' ITEMS ⚘

Bobby Moore scored two goals for England in 108 appearances:

v Poland at Anfield on 5 January 1966 – England drew 1–1
v Norway in Oslo on 29 June 1966 – England won 6–1

✥ THE LIONS ROAR (10) ✥

"We used to sing 'Three Lions', the Skinner and Baddiel song, for a laugh on the team coach. Gazza had it blaring out of his room at all hours of the day and night."
Robbie Fowler *on England's Euro 96 preparations.*

✥ SUPERSUB ✥

Teddy Sheringham holds the record for the highest number of substitute appearances for England – 21.

✥ WORTH THE WAIT ✥

Ian Callaghan made his international debut for England against France on 20 July 1966. However, he did not win his second England cap until 11 years later, when he was recalled by Ron Greenwood to play against Switzerland on 7 September 1977. This is the record gap between games for an England player, excluding games missed by players as a result of either World War.

✥ PETER BEARDSLEY ✥

During his football career, Peter played for Carlisle United, Vancouver Whitecaps (two spells), Manchester United, Newcastle United (two spells), Liverpool, Everton, Manchester City (on loan), Fulham (on loan) and Hartlepool United. Peter won 59 caps for England, scoring nine times. Kevin Keegan once said of Peter: "Peter is simply the best, better than all the rest."

With the £1.9 million that Newcastle United received from Liverpool for Peter Beardsley in 1987, the club was able to help finance the building of the Jackie Milburn Stand at St James's Park.

✥ ENGLAND U-TURN ✥

Prior to an England international trial game on 21 January 1914 at Sunderland, Bolton Wanderers' Alex Donaldson admitted that he was actually born in Scotland. Charles Wallace of Aston Villa took his place in the match, and Donaldson ended up in the Scottish side that beat England 3–1 at Hampden Park on 4 April 1914[†]. In total, Donaldson made six appearances for Scotland from 1914 to 1922.

[†]This was England's last official international match prior to the outbreak of the First World War.

⚔️ ZIEG HEIL INDIGNITY ⚔️

This match is remembered more for the England team's giving the Nazi salute during the pre-game ceremonies in Berlin's packed Olympic Stadium on 14 May 1938, than it is for the 6–3 thumping England gave the Nazi regime's sporting pride and joy that day.[†] The game was Germany's last match before the 1938 World Cup Finals in France, and after a 16-match unbeaten run of 10 straight games the Germans were full of confidence.

Prior to the kick-off, at the direction of the British Ambassador to Germany, Sir Neville Henderson, who was supported by Stanley Rous, the Secretary of the FA, the England players joined in the raised arm fascist salute as the German national anthem was being played, while Nazi leaders Goering, Goebbels, Hess and von Ribbentrop watched.

Only captain Eddie Hapgood and Cliff Bastin had made more than ten international appearances for England prior to the game. Indeed England's left-half, Don Welsh, and centre-forward, Frank Broome, were making their debuts whilst the inside-right, Jackie Robinson, was only winning his second cap. Subsequently, in the seven years between 24 May 1939 and 28 September 1946 England did not play any official internationals. Of the England team that played in Berlin on 14 May 1938, only Stanley Matthews wore the England colours after World War II. The England team that day in Berlin was:

1. Vic Woodley................................*Chelsea*
2. Bert Sproston........................*Leeds United*
3. Eddie Hapgood *(captain)* ....*Arsenal*
4. Ken Willingham.......*Huddersfield Town*
5. Alf Young................*Huddersfield Town*
6. Don Welsh................*Charlton Athletic*
7. Stanley Matthews................*Stoke City*
8. Jackie Robinson........*Sheffield Wednesday*
9. Frank Broome ....*Aston Villa*
10. Len Goulden................*West Ham United*
11. Cliff Bastin................................*Arsenal*

Scorers: Bastin 12 mins (0–1), Gauchel 20 mins (1–1), Robinson 26 mins (1–2), Broome 36 mins (1–3), Matthews, 39 mins (1–4), Gellesch 42 mins (2–4), Robinson 50 mins (2–5), Pesser 70 mins (3–5) and Goulden 72 mins (3–6). *Attendance:* 103,000.

[†] *During England's 6-3 humiliation of the "master race" Sir Neville Henderson, the British Ambassador, offered his binoculars to Hermann Goering saying: "What marvellous goals – you really should take a look at them."*

ENGLAND XI – ASTON VILLA

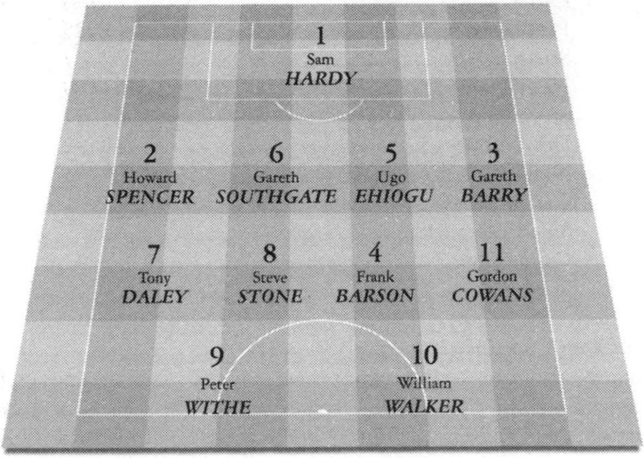
1
Sam
HARDY
2
Howard
SPENCER
6
Gareth
SOUTHGATE
5
Ugo
EHIOGU
3
Gareth
BARRY
7
Tony
DALEY
8
Steve
STONE
4
Frank
BARSON
11
Gordon
COWANS
9
Peter
WITHE
10
William
WALKER

Substitutes

David *JAMES*, Earl *BARRETT*, Lee *HENDRIE*,
Paul *MERSON*, Darius *VASSELL*

Manager

Graham *TAYLOR*

Did You Know That?

The club was formed in 1874 as the Cricketers of Villa Cross Wesleyan Church. Villa's first match was against Aston Brook St Mary's rugby side and as a condition of the match, they had to agree to play the first half under rugby rules and the second half under football rules. Villa won the game 1–0.

THE SHORTEST EVER ENGLAND CAREER

Brighton & Hove Albion's Peter Ward played the last five minutes of England's 2–1 win over Australia in Sydney on 31 May 1980, but never appeared in an England shirt again.

MOST WINS AS MANAGER

England won 78 of the 139 games they played under Walter Winterbottom. The next best winning record is held by Sir Alf Ramsey with 69 wins from 113 outings.

⚜ ENGLAND'S LAST 10 FOREST REDS ⚜

Player	Years
Peter Davenport	1985
Stuart Pearce	1987–97
Neil Webb	1987–89
Steve Hodge	1988–91
Des Walker	1988–92
Nigel Clough	1989–93
Gary Charles	1991
Stan Collymore	1995
Colin Cooper	1995
Steve Stone	1995–96

Did You Know That?
Four Nottingham Forest players were in the starting line-up for England against Sweden on 10 June 1979. Viv Anderson, Trevor Francis, Peter Shilton and Tony Woodcock were part of Forest's 1979 European Cup winning team that played in England's 0–0 draw in Stockholm that day. A total of 37 Nottingham Forest players have been capped by England.

⚜ PYJAMA GAME ⚜

For the first time ever England's new kit manufactured by Admiral in 1974 had embellishments on it other than the three lions emblem. Red and blue striping appeared on both the collar and the sleeves, leading former England centre-forward Jimmy Greaves to comment that the striping made the new shirt look like pyjamas. The new colourful shirt design, and the appearance of the Admiral logo, were the direct result of a new commercial arrangement under which Admiral paid royalties to the Football Association for the right to promote and sell replica England kits.

⚜ WORLD CUP WILLIE ⚜

World Cup Willie became the first official World Cup mascot during the 1966 World Cup finals.

⚜ ONE GOAL IN 86 GAMES ⚜

Kenny Samson played 86 times for England but only scored one goal, v Finland, in a 5–0 win at Wembley on 17 October 1984.

⚜

⟋ WORLD CUP FINALS – MEXICO 1986 ⟋

In 1986, Mexico staged the World Cup for the second time, thereby becoming the first country to host two World Cup finals. England opened their campaign with a 1–0 defeat by Portugal followed by a disappointing 0–0 draw with Morocco. Then England beat Poland 3–0 thanks to a Gary Lineker hat-trick. All of England's opening group games were played in Estadio Tecnológico, Monterrey. England finished second in the group and qualified for the second round.

England's opponents in the second round were Paraguay in Estadio Azteca, Mexico City. Two goals from Gary Lineker and one from Peter Beardsley gave England a 3–0 win and passage to the quarter-finals. Argentina stood between England and a place in the semi-finals but the infamous "Hand of God" goal from Diego Maradona put an end to England's dream. England lost 2–1 in Estadio Azteca with Gary Lineker scoring his 6th goal of the tournament, the most number of goals scored by an England player at a World Cup finals. Argentina went on to win the World Cup beating West Germany 3–2 in the final, with goals from Brown, Valdano and Burruchaga.

FIRST ROUND, GROUP F

MONTERREY, 3 JUNE 1986, 23,000

Portugal (0) 1   v   **England** (0) 0
(Carlos Manuel 76)

England: Shilton, Stevens G., Sansom, Butcher, Fenwick, Hoddle, Robson (Hodge, 79), Wilkins, Waddle (Beardsley, 79), Hateley, Lineker.

MONTERREY, 6 JUNE 1986, 33,500

England (0) 0   v   **Morocco** (0) 0

England: Shilton, Stevens G., Sansom, Butcher, Fenwick, Hoddle, Robson (Hodge, 4), Wilkins, Waddle, Hateley (Stevens G.A., 76), Lineker.

MONTERREY, 11 JUNE 1986, 23,000

England (3) 3   v   **Poland** (0) 0
(Lineker 9, 14, 34)

England: Shilton, Stevens G., Sansom, Butcher, Fenwick, Hoddle, Reid, Steven, Hodge, Beardsley (Waddle, 75), Lineker (Beardsley, 85).

Group F – Final table

	P	W	D	L	F	A	Pts
Morocco	3	1	2	0	3	1	4
England	3	1	1	1	3	1	3
Poland	3	1	0	2	1	3	2
Portugal	3	1	0	2	2	4	2

SECOND ROUND

MEXICO CITY, 18 JUNE 1986, 98,728

England (1) 3   v   **Paraguay (0) 0**
(Lineker 31, 73,
Beardsley 56)

England: Seaman, Shilton, Stevens G., Sansom, Martin, Butcher,
Hoddle, Reid (Stevens G.A., 58), Steven, Hodge,
Beardsley (Hateley, 80), Lineker.

QUARTER-FINAL

MEXICO CITY, 22 JUNE 1986, 114,580

Argentina (0) 2   v   **England (0) 1**
(Maradona 51, 54)   (Lineker 80)

England: Shilton, Stevens G., Sansom, Butcher, Fenwick,
Hoddle, Reid (Waddle, 64), Hodge, Steven (Barnes, 74),
Beardsley, Lineker.

England's 1998 World Cup Finals Squad

1 Peter Shilton ....*(Southampton)*
2 Gary Stevens ....*(Everton)*
3 Kenny Sansom ....*(Arsenal)*
4 Glenn Hoddle ....*(Spurs)*
5 Alvin Martin ....*(West Ham)*
6 Terry Butcher ...... *(Ipswich Town)*
7 Bryan Robson............*(Man Utd)*
8 Ray Wilkins ....*(AC Milan)*
9 Mark Hateley ....*(AC Milan)*
10 Gary Lineker ....*(Everton)*
11 Chris Waddle ....*(Spurs)*

12 Viv Anderson ....*(Arsenal)*
13 Chris Woods........*(Norwich City)*
14 Terry Fenwick ....*(QPR)*
15 Gary Stevens ....*(Spurs)*
16 Peter Reid ....*(Everton)*
17 Trevor Steven ....*(Everton)*
18 Steve Hodge...........*(Aston Villa)*
19 John Barnes.................*(Watford)*
20 Peter Beardsley...*(Newcastle Utd)*
21 Kerry Dixon.................*(Chelsea)*
22 Gary Bailey ....*(Man Utd)*

Manager: Bobby Robson

Did You Know That?

Gary Lineker's six goals in the tournament earned him the 1986
World Cup Golden Boot Award.

⚜

⚓ DAVID BECKHAM, OBE ⚓

David Robert Joseph Beckham was born on 2 May 1975 in Leytonstone, London. When he was a schoolboy, David attended Tottenham Hotspur's School of Excellence. In 1989, he signed schoolboy forms with Manchester United and became a trainee on 8 July 1991. On 23 September 1992, David made his United debut in a Rumbelows Cup tie at Brighton & Hove Albion.

At the end of the 1995–96 season, a David Beckham inspired United became the first English Football League Club to win the coveted "Double" twice, following their all conquering 1993–94 season. On the opening day of the 1996–97 season, David scored perhaps the greatest FA Premier League goal of all time. United visited Wimbledon at Selhurst Park and David sensationally chipped Neil Sullivan in the Wimbledon goal from 55 yards.

On 1 September 1996, David made his international debut for England in a 3–1 World Cup qualifying game away to Moldova. However, during the 1998 World Cup finals in France, David was placed before the TV cameras by Glenn Hoddle after being dropped for England's opening game against Tunisia, and was then sent off against Argentina in a game England lost 4–3 in a penalty shoot-out in St Etienne, a result that eliminated England from the competition. Many England fans and journalists blamed Beckham for England's elimination from the competition. He became the target of severe media criticism and much public abuse. Undaunted, Beckham was instrumental in helping Manchester United to do the "Treble" of Premier League, FA Cup and Champions League in 1999. When Kevin Keegan vacated the England team manager's role in October 2000, caretaker manager, Peter Taylor, made David the England captain, a position he still holds today.

On 6 October 2001, Beckham almost single-handedly ensured England reached the 2002 World Cup finals. In their final qualifying game, England were trailing Greece 2–1 at Old Trafford with just seconds remaining. Beckham stepped up to fire home an injury time equalizer to book England's place at the finals in Japan/South Korea. At the following summer's finals, Beckham and England gained revenge on Argentina for putting them out of the 1998 World Cup finals, when Beckham scored from the penalty spot to give England a 1–0 win over their South American rivals in Sapporo, Japan. On 12 November 2005, David captained England for the 50th time in their 3–2 friendly win over Argentina in Geneva, Switzerland. In July 2005, David was part of the team that won the right for London to host the 2012 Olympic Games.

⚜

⚯ ENGLAND'S LAST 10 SPURS ⚮

Player	Years
Sol Campbell	1996–2001
Ian Walker	1996–97
Les Ferdinand	1997–98
Tim Sherwood	1999
Ledley King	2002–present
Jermain Defoe	2004–present
Anthony Gardner	2004
Paul Robinson	2004–present
Michael Carrick	2005–present
Jermaine Jenas	2005–present

Did You Know That?
Four Spurs players have appeared for England in the same game on four separate occasions. The first occurrence was on 19 April 1921 against Scotland when Bert Bliss, Jimmy Dimmock, Arthur Grimsdell (captain) and Bert Smith all played in England's 3–0 defeat at Hampden Park. The last occurrence was when Darren Anderton, Sol Campbell, Teddy Sheringham and Ian Walker played against Hungary on 18 May 1996. A total of 57 Spurs players have been capped by England.

⚯ ENGLAND'S SCOTTISH INDIAN ⚮

William Lindsay, born in India on 3 August 1847, won his only England cap in the 3–1 defeat to Scotland played at the Kennington Oval on 3 March 1877. He had previously played for Scotland in five unofficial internationals: the 1–1 draw on 5 March 1870, the 1–0 England victory on 19 November 1870, the 1–1 draw on 25 February 1871, the 2–1 England win on 18 November 1871 and the 1–0 England win on 24 February 1872. Prior to the formation of the Scottish Football Association in 1873, the Scotland team for unofficial internationals was drawn from London-based Scots plus a few "all-comers" needed to make up the numbers.

⚯ THERE BY RIGHT ⚮

When England qualified for 1982 finals, it was the first time England had qualified for the World Cup finals in 20 years. In 1966 they qualified as the host nation; they were the reigning World Champions in 1970, but failed to qualify in both 1974 and 1978.

⟡ THE LIONS ROAR (11) ⟡

"I only went in for a filling and I came out drunk – it must have been some anaesthetic! But get the video tapes of that tournament and you'll see how successful the dentist's chair was!"
Paul Gascoigne *recalling an infamous England squad drinking session prior to Euro 96.*

⟡ ENGLAND'S YOUTH POLICY ⟡

England's six youngest capped players are:

Wayne Rooney (Everton) 17-years and 111 days
James Prinsep (Clapham Rovers) 17-years and 253 days
Thurston Rostron (Darwen) 17-years and 312 days
Clement Mitchell (Upton Park) 18-years and 24 days
Michael Owen (Liverpool) 18-years and 59 days
Duncan Edwards (Manchester United) 18-years and 184 days

⟡ LEFT OUT IN THE COLD ⟡

Paul Goddard is the only player to make his England debut as a substitute, score and then never be picked again. He scored against Iceland in Reykjavik on 2 June 1982 in a friendly before the 1982 World Cup finals in Spain. Paul came on as a substitute for the injured Cyrille Regis, and latched on to a through ball by Glenn Hoddle to score England's equalizer in the 69th minute in a 1–1 draw.

⟡ ENGLAND SUB SCORES TWICE ⟡

Nat Lofthouse of Bolton Wanderers was the first substitute to score two goals in an international for England. He came on as a substitute for Manchester United's Tommy Taylor and scored twice in England's 5–1 win over Finland in Helsinki on 20 May 1956. Six months later Taylor himself replaced Johnny Haynes of Fulham in the friendly against Yugoslavia, at Wembley on 28 November, and scored two goals.

⟡ HUNGARY FOR SUCCESS ⟡

Hungary beat England 6–3 at Wembley on 25 November 1953 and 7–1 in Budapest a year later. Between 1950 and 1956 the Hungarians lost just one international match.

⊕

⌒ RECORD ENGLAND APPEARANCES ⌒

Player	Clubs/Career	Caps	Gls
Peter Shilton	Leicester City, Stoke City, Nottingham Forest, Southampton, Derby County, 1971–90	125	0
Bobby Moore	West Ham Utd, 1962–74	108	2
Bobby Charlton	Man Utd, 1958–70	106	49
Billy Wright	Wolves, 1947–59	105	3
Bryan Robson	WBA, Man Utd, 1980–92	90	26
Kenny Sansom	Crystal Palace, Arsenal, 1979–88	86	1
Ray Wilkins	Chelsea, Man Utd, Milan, 1976–87	84	3
David Beckham*	Man Utd, Real Madrid 1996–present	82 82	16 16
Gary Lineker	Leicester City, Everton, Barcelona, Spurs, 1984–92	80	48
John Barnes	Watford, Liverpool, 1983–95	79	11
Stuart Pearce	Nottingham Forest, West Ham Utd, 1987–99	78	4
Terry Butcher	Ipswich Town, Rangers, 1980–90	77	3
Tom Finney	Preston North End, 1947–59	76	30
Gary Neville	Man Utd, 1995–present	76	0
David Seaman	QPR, Arsenal, 1989–2002	75	0

*Up to and including the Denmark game on 17 August 2005.

⌒ ENGLAND'S FIRST SUBSTITUTE ⌒

On 18 May 1950 Jimmy Mullen of Wolverhampton Wanderers became England's first ever substitute when he came on for Jackie Milburn (Newcastle United) after just 11 minutes in England's 4–1 win over Belgium in Brussels. In the same game Mullen also became the first England substitute to score in an international.

⌒ KICK IT OUT ⌒

When England played Spain away on 17 November 2004, Ashley Cole and Shaun Wright-Phillips had to endure abusive racist chants from sections of the Spanish crowd. Spain won 1–0 with a goal from Asier del Horno.

✧ NAME CHANGE ✧

Frederick Patey Chappell, who was born in England, changed his name to Frederick Brunning Maddison in 1873, having played for England in the first official international in 1872 against Scotland. However, he had already played for Scotland in the 1–1 draw on 25 February 1871, the third unofficial international involving England and Scotland.

✧ HIT FOR 7 TWICE ✧

England have twice conceded seven goals in an international. Scotland beat England 7–2 in Glasgow on 2 March 1878, and Hungary won 7–1 in Budapest on 23 May 1954. The 7–1 loss to Hungary also represents England's biggest ever margin of defeat.

✧ MOST GOALS SCORED WHEN BEATEN ✧

England once scored four goals in a game but still lost the match. Scotland beat England 5–4 in the first Hampden Park game between the two sides on 13 March 1880. A year earlier England had beaten Scotland at the Kennington Oval by the same score.

✧ PROMISING START ✧

Tommy Lawton of Chelsea scored the fastest England goal in history. He scored after just 17 seconds in England's 10-0 friendly win over Portugal in Lisbon on 27 May 1947.

✧ THE FIRST ENGLAND DISMISSAL ✧

Alan Mullery of Spurs was the first England player to be shown the red card in an international when he was dismissed against Yugoslavia in Florence on 5 June 1968.

✧ THE HIGHEST SCORING DRAW ✧

The highest scoring England draw is 4–4. England have managed that 4–4 scoreline twice, against the Rest of Europe at Wembley on 21 October 1953, and against Belgium, after extra time, at the 1954 World Cup finals in Switzerland on 17 June 1954.[†]

[†] *England have also played in six 3–3 draws, the last occasion being against Sweden at Elland Road in the Umbro Cup International Challenge Tournament on 8 June 1995.*

⚜

~ ENGLAND'S LAST 10 VILLANS ~

Player	Years
Kevin Richardson	1994
Gareth Southgate	1995–2002
Ugo Ehiogu	1996
Stan Collymore	1997
Dion Dublin	1998
Paul Merson	1998
Lee Hendrie	1998
Gareth Barry	2000–03
David James	2001
Darius Vassell	2002–04

Did You Know That?
In Peter Taylor's solitary match in charge of England three Aston Villa players were in the starting 11 for the first time since 1931. David James, Gareth Barry and Gareth Southgate all played against Italy on 13 November 2000. A total of 64 Aston Villa players have been capped by England, the highest number of England internationals from any club up to the end of 2005.

~ ALEX THE SCOT ~

Alexander Morten, the England goalkeeper when they beat Scotland 4–2 in England's second official international at the Kennington Oval on 8 March 1873, appeared for Scotland in the first unofficial international between the two countries, the 1–1 draw on 5 March 1870.

~ THEY SHOOT, HE SAVES ~

The last England goalkeeper to save a penalty in open play was Paul Robinson who denied Spain at the Bernabeu Stadium, Madrid, on 17 November 2004 in a game England lost 1–0.

~ SCOTS FIRST TO BEAT ENGLAND ~

Scotland were the first country to beat England in an international, winning 2–1 in Glasgow on 7 March 1874.[†]

[†]*The first football international played without involving a British side was between the United States and Canada, played in Newark, New Jersey, USA on 28 November 1885. The Canadians won 1–0.*

✑ EUROPEAN CHAMPIONSHIP 1988 ✑

Having failed to qualify for the final stages of the 1984 tournament, England participated in their third European Championship finals in West Germany in 1988. England were drawn in Group 2 with Holland, the Republic of Ireland and the USSR. England lost their opening game 1–0 to the Republic of Ireland in the Neckarstadion, Stuttgart, and lost their next game 3–1 to Holland in the Rheinstadion, Düsseldorf, and lost their final group game 3–1 in Waldstadion, Frankfurt to the USSR. The USSR topped the group followed by Holland and the Republic of Ireland as England finished bottom.

Holland and the USSR went on to contest the 1988 Final in the Olympiastadion, Munich, with the Dutch winning 2–0. Holland's Marco van Basten, who had scored a hat-trick in the 3–1 win over England, was voted the Player of the Tournament.

FIRST ROUND, GROUP 2
12 JUNE 1988, STUTTGART, 51,373

England (0) **0**   v   **Republic of Ireland** (1) **1**
                             (Houghton 6)

England: Shilton, Stevens G., Wright, Adams, Sansom, Waddle, Webb (Hoddle, 61), Robson, Barnes, Beardsley (Hateley, 81), Lineker.

---

15 JUNE 1988, DUSSELDORF, 63,940

England (0) **1**   v   **Holland** (1) **3**
(Robson 53)   (Van Basten 44, 71, 75)

England: Shilton, Stevens G., Wright, Adams, Sansom, Stevens G.A., (Waddle, 69), Hoddle, Robson, Barnes, Beardsley (Hateley, 74), Lineker.

---

18 JUNE 1988, FRANKFURT, 48,335

England (1) **1**   v   **Soviet Union** (2) **3**
(Adams 16)   (Aleinikov 3,
                             Mikhailichenko 28,
                             Pasulko 73)

England: Woods, Stevens G., Watson, Adams, Sansom, Steven, McMahon (Webb, 53), Robson, Hoddle, Lineker (Hateley, 64), Barnes.

Group 2 – Final table

	P	W	D	L	F	A	Pts
Soviet Union	3	2	1	0	5	2	5
Holland	3	1	0	1	4	2	4
Rep of Ireland	3	1	1	1	2	2	3
England	3	0	0	3	2	7	0

England's 1988 European Championship Finals Squad

1 Peter Shilton............*(Derby County)*	11 John Barnes......................*(Liverpool)*
2 Gary Stevens.....................*(Everton)*	12 Chris Waddle........................*(Spurs)*
3 Kenny Sansom.................*(Arsenal)*	13 Chris Woods....................*(Rangers)*
4 Neil Webb..................*(Notts Forest)*	14 Viv Anderson..................*(Man Utd)*
5 Dave Watson.....................*(Everton)*	15 Steve McMahon.............*(Liverpool)*
6 Tony Adams......................*(Arsenal)*	16 Peter Reid..........................*(Everton)*
7 Bryan Robson ....*(Man Utd)*	17 Glenn Hoddle......... *(AS Monaco)*
8 Trevor Steven.................*(Everton)*	18 Mark Hateley............*(AS Monaco)*
9 Peter Beardsley.............*(Liverpool)*	19 Mark Wright........*(Derby County)*
10 Gary Lineker..................*(Barcelona)*	20 Tony Dorigo.......................*(Chelsea)*

Manager: Bobby Robson

～ OFFICIALLY UNOFFICIAL ～

Arnold Kirke-Smith, born in Ecclesfield near Sheffield on 23 April 1850, was capped by England in the first official international, the scoreless draw with Scotland in 1872. He also played for Scotland in the third and fourth unofficial international matches between the two countries: the 1–1 draw on 25 February 1871 and the 2–1 England win on 18 November 1871.

～ ENGLAND STALWART ～

When Terry Venables of Chelsea made his full international debut for England against Belgium in a 2–2 draw on 21 October 1964 at Wembley, he became the first player to appear for England at every level: schoolboy, amateur, youth, under-23 and full international level. He also managed the England team.

～ BROWN'S THE NAME ～

Brown is the most common surname for an England international with a total of nine "Browns" having played for England: Anthony Brown, Arthur Brown (2), George Brown, James Brown, John Brown, Kenneth Brown, Wes Brown and William Brown.

⟋ NO PLACE LIKE HOME ⟍

Wembley (Empire Stadium) did not become England's "official home" until January 1966. Here is a list of the grounds in England where internationals have been played both prior to 1966 and after Wembley was closed to make way for the new Wembley Stadium:

Alexandra Meadows, Blackburn ❖ Anfield, Liverpool
Ayresome Park, Middlesbrough ❖ Ashton Gate, Bristol City
The Baseball Ground, Derby ❖ Bloomfield Road, Blackpool
Brammall Lane, Sheffield ❖ City of Manchester Stadium, Manchester
The City Ground, Nottingham ❖ County Ground, Derby
Craven Cottage, Fulham ❖ The Crystal Palace, Sydenham
The Dell, Southampton ❖ The Den, Millwall ❖ Elland Road, Leeds
Ewood Park, Blackburn ❖ Fratton Park, Portsmouth
Goodison Park, Liverpool ❖ The Hawthorns, West Bromwich
Highbury, London ❖ Hillsbrough, Sheffield
Kennington Oval, London ❖ Leamington Road, Blackburn
Leeds Road, Huddersfield ❖ Liverpool Cricket Club, Aigburth
Maine Road, Manchester ❖ Molineux, Wolverhampton
Newcastle Road, Sunderland ❖ Nantwich Road, Crewe
Old Trafford, Manchester ❖ Park Avenue, Bradford
Perry Barr, Birmingham ❖ Pride Park, Derby ❖ Queen's Club, London
Richmond Athletic Ground ❖ Riverside Stadium, Middlesbrough
Roker Park, Sunderland ❖ St James's Park, Newcastle
St Mary's, Southampton ❖ Selhurst Park, London
Stadium of Light, Sunderland ❖ Stamford Bridge, Chelsea, London
Trent Bridge, Nottingham ❖ Turf Moor, Burnley
Upton Park, London ❖ Victoria Ground, Stoke
Villa Park, Birmingham ❖ The Walkers Stadium, Leicester
Whalley Range, Manchester ❖ White Hart Lane, London

⟋ SHILTON IS ROBSON'S NO. 1 ⟍

Peter Shilton was the player most capped by Bobby Robson during his spell as England manager. Bobby awarded Peter 83 caps.

⟋ WORLD CUP MULTIPLE-GOALSCORER ⟍

Gary Lineker is the only England player to have more than one multiple-goal game at the World Cup finals. Gary scored a hat-trick against Poland and two goals against Paraguay during the 1986 finals in Mexico, and he scored two against Cameroon, both from the penalty spot, at Italia '90.

✧ STAR-SPANGLED BOBBY ✧

Bobby Moore, who made 108 appearances for England, 70 as captain, played for Team America against Italy, Brazil and England in the USA Bicentennial Cup Tournament in 1976. The USA team was called Team America because the official USA National side was not then strong enough to meet top-flight opposition and they called upon some of the North American Soccer League (NASL) stars who no longer played for their own countries. At the time Bobby was playing for San Antonio Thunder.

✧ THREE GOALS AND NO WINS ✧

England have scored three goals and lost on four occasions: 5–3 against Wales at the Racecourse Ground in Wrexham on 13 March 1882; 4–3 against Spain in Madrid on 15 May 1929; 6–3 against Hungary at Wembley Stadium on 25 November 1953, and 4–3 against Austria in Vienna on 13 June 1979.

✧ MOST GOALS CONCEDED IN A WIN ✧

England have conceded four goals and still won the match on three occasions, and each time by a 5–4 scoreline. England beat Scotland 5–4 at the Kennington Oval on 5 April 1879, Scotland again at Hillsborough in Sheffield on 10 April 1920, and Czechoslovakia at White Hart Lane on 1 December 1937.

✧ LINEKER HITS THE TARGET ✧

Gary Lineker scored in six World Cup finals matches, against Poland, Paraguay and Argentina at the 1986 tournament in Mexico, and against the Republic of Ireland, Cameroon and West Germany at the 1990 tournament in Italy.

✧ THE RUSSIAN LINESMAN ✧

Tofik Bakhramov[†] was the Russian (he was actually born in Azerbaijan) linesman in the 1966 World Cup Final who declared that Geoff Hurst's shot that hit the underside of the crossbar, had crossed the goal line – and the rest, as they say, is history.

[†] *The Tofig Bakhramov Stadium, Baku, where England beat Azerbaijan 1–0 on 13 October 2004, was named after the linesman who made the controversial decision in the 1966 World Cup Final.*

⚜

⟋ GARY LINEKER, OBE ⟍

Gary Winston Lineker was born on 30 November 1960 in Leicester. Gary signed for Leicester City in 1976 and in 1978 he made his senior debut for the club. In 1980 he won the Second Division Championship with the Filbert Street side. He won the first of his 80 England caps on 26 May 1984, coming on as a substitute for Tony Woodcock in England's 1–1 draw with Scotland at Hampden Park.

Gary played for the Foxes for seven years before siging for Everton in the summer of 1985 for £800,000. His first and only season with the Toffees saw him rise to national fame, scoring 40 goals in 42 games during the 1985–86 season. However, despite Gary's impressive goals tally Everton were unable to defend the First Division Championship which they'd won the previous season, falling just two points short of city rivals, Liverpool. To add insult to injury, Liverpool won the "Double", beating Everton 3–1 in the FA Cup Final at Wembley, with Gary scoring in the game. Such was the impact that Gary made on Merseyside during the 1985–86 season, he was voted both the PFA Player of the Year and the Football Writers' Player of the Year. At the end of the season Barcelona made Everton an offer they could not refuse and Gary signed for the Catalan club.

Gary won the Golden Boot award at Mexico '86 as a Barcelona player. In total Gary played 99 times for Barcelona scoring 44 times, winning the Spanish Cup in 1988 and the European Cup Winners' Cup in 1989. In the summer of 1989, Gary returned to England and joined Tottenham Hotspur. Gary stayed at White Hart Lane for three seasons winning the FA Cup with the north London club in 1991, managed by future England manager, Terry Venables. In total, Gary played 105 games for Spurs and scored 67 goals. Gary helped England to the 1990 World Cup semi-finals and when he retired from international football, Gary had scored 48 goals in 80 games for England, one fewer than Bobby Charlton's England record of 49 goals (although Charlton took 26 more caps to score his extra goal). After Spurs, Gary moved to Japan, where he endured an injury-plagued spell in the Japanese J. League with Nagoya Grampus Eight managed by Arsène Wenger.

Despite his long career, Gary was never given a card by a referee. When he retired from playing, Gary began his media career, initially as a football pundit before replacing Des Lynam as the BBC's anchorman for "Match of the Day". Gary has also been a team captain on the sports game show, "They Think It's All Over" and appeared on many TV adverts for Walker's Crisps.

⚜ THEY SHALL NOT PASS ⚜

Peter Shilton is England's No. 1 goalkeeper for World Cup shut-outs with 10 clean sheets in 17 games at the 1982, 1986 and 1990 World Cup finals. Gordon Banks is in second place with six clean sheets in nine games (1966 and 1970), whilst David Seaman is third with five clean sheets in nine games (1998 and 2002).

⚜ THE LIONS ROAR (12) ⚜

"The nice aspect of football captaincy is that the manager gets the blame if things go wrong."
Gary Lineker on being made England captain in 1990.

⚜ THE MOST SUBBED PLAYER ⚜

In his 66 appearances for England, Paul Scholes was substituted 38 times.

⚜ A VILLANOUS BUNCH ⚜

Up to the end of the 2004–05 season, Aston Villa have provided 64 England international players, a record number from any club.

⚜ THE NEVILLE BROTHERS ⚜

Up to the end of the 2004–05 season, Gary and Phil Neville have started 11 England games together.

⚜ FIVE ASSISTS ⚜

Of Malcolm Macdonald's five goals against Cyprus in England's 5–0 win at Wembley on 16 April 1975, Mick Channon set up every single one.

⚜ MASTERS OF THE SCORELESS DRAW ⚜

England have been involved in eight 0–0 draws at the finals of the World Cup: 0–0 v Brazil (1958), 0–0 v Bulgaria (1962), 0–0 v Uruguay (1966), 0–0 v West Germany (1982), 0–0 v Spain (1982), 0–0 v Morocco (1986), 0–0 v Holland (1990) and 0–0 v Nigeria (2002). That makes a total of eight scoreless draws in 50 World Cup finals games, or one in every six played.

⭑ ENGLAND XI – NEWCASTLE UNITED ⭑

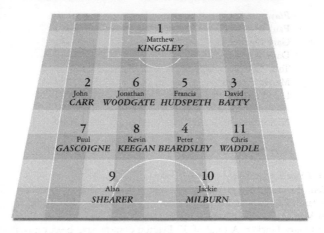

1
Matthew
KINGSLEY

2
John
CARR

6
Jonathan
WOODGATE

5
Francis
HUDSPETH

3
David
BATTY

7
Paul
GASCOIGNE

8
Kevin
KEEGAN

4
Peter
BEARDSLEY

11
Chris
WADDLE

9
Alan
SHEARER

10
Jackie
MILBURN

Substitutes
Warren *BARTON*, Steve *HOWEY*, Jonathan *WOODGATE*,
Les *FERDINAND*, Michael *OWEN*
Manager
Sir Bobby *ROBSON CBE*

Did You Know That?
Newcastle United began life as Newcastle East End from 1882–92.
When Newcastle West End was wound up in 1892, some of its
players and most of its backroom staff joined East End. East End also
took over the lease on St James' Park and in December 1892, East
End became Newcastle United.

⭑ ENGLAND'S FIRST CENTURION ⭑

Billy Wright was the first player to win 100 international caps for
England.

⭑ THE CAT'S ONE WORLD CUP GAME ⭑

When Gordon Banks was taken ill before England's quarter-final
game against West Germany in Mexico in 1970, Peter Bonetti
replaced him in the starting line-up. It was Bonetti's only appearance
in a World Cup finals game and his last ever game for his country.

⚜ ENGLAND'S LAST 10 TOFFEES ⚜

Player	Years
Paul Bracewell	1985
Gary Lineker	1985–86
Dave Watson	1987–88
Tony Cottee	1988–89
Martin Keown	1992
David Unsworth	1995
Andy Hinchcliffe	1996–97
Nicky Barmby	2000
Michael Ball	2001
Wayne Rooney	2003–04

Did You Know That?

Four Everton players featured in the same England side against Poland, Paraguay and Argentina during the 1986 World Cup finals in Mexico. The four were Gary Stevens, Trevor Steven, Peter Reid and Gary Lineker. A total of 57 Everton players have been capped by England.

⚜ EURO 2008 DRAW ⚜

England were drawn against Andorra, Croatia, Estonia, Israel, FYR Macedonia and Russia in Group E of the qualifying competition for Euro 2008. England will be playing Andorra and Estonia for the first time, and it will also be their first competitive games against Israel and Russia (although England did previously play against Russia when it was known as the USSR.)

⚜ SHEAR MISS ⚜

During his international career, Alan Shearer only missed one penalty for England. He hit the post in a World Cup qualifier in Poland on 31 May 1997.

⚜ ENGLAND'S FIRST FOREIGN VISITORS ⚜

On 19 March 1923 Belgium became the first foreign national side to visit England when the two sides met at Arsenal Stadium. England won 6–1. In the 82 years since England first played Belgium, the two countries have only met a further 19 times, with England winning 13, drawing five and losing just one.

⟋ WORLD CUP FINALS – ITALY 1990 ⟍

In the first phase of Italia '90, England were drawn in Group F with Egypt, Holland and the Republic of Ireland. England drew 1–1 with the Republic of Ireland, drew 0–0 with Holland and beat Egypt 1–0 to end up top of their group.

On 26 June, England beat Belgium 1–0 in Stadio Renato Dall'Ara, Bologna thanks to a goal in the last minute of extra-time to progress to the quarter-finals for the second World Cup in succession. In the quarter-finals England narrowly squeezed past Cameroon with a 3–2 victory after extra-time. Now only West Germany stood between England and their first Final appearance since 1966. The game was played in Stadio Delle Alpi, Turin, and after 90 minutes the score was 1–1. Extra-time could not separate the sides and the game ended 1–1 with the winner to be decided in a penalty shoot-out. England lost the resulting shoot-out 4–3, with Stuart Pearce and Chris Waddle both missing from the spot. England lost the third-place play-off game to the host nation, Italy, 2–1 in Stadio San Nicola, Bari, whilst West Germany beat Argentina 1–0 in the Final.

FIRST ROUND, GROUP F

CAGLIARI, 11 JUNE 1990, 35,238

England (1) 1   v   **Republic of Ireland** (0) 1
(Lineker 8)   (Sheedy 73)

England: Shilton, Stevens, Pearce, Walker, Butcher, Waddle, Robson, Gascoigne, Barnes, Beardsley (McMahon, 69), Lineker (Bull, 83).

CAGLIARI, 16 JUNE 1990, 35,267

England (0) 0   v   **Holland** (0) 0

England: Shilton, Parker, Pearce, Walker, Butcher, Wright, Robson (Platt, 64), Waddle (Bull, 58), Gascoigne, Barnes, Lineker.

CAGLIARI, 21 JUNE 1990, 34,959

England (0) 1   v   **Egypt** (0) 0
(Wright 64)

England: Shilton, Parker, Pearce, Walker, Wright, Waddle (Platt, 86), McMahon, Gascoigne, Barnes, Lineker, Bull (Beardsley, 84).

Group F – Final table

	P	W	D	L	F	A	Pts
England	3	1	2	0	2	1	5
Holland	3	0	3	0	2	2	3
Ireland Republic	3	0	3	0	2	2	3
Egypt	3	0	2	1	1	2	2

SECOND ROUND

BOLOGNA, 26 JUNE 1990, 34,520

England (0) 1   **v**   **Belgium (0) 0**
(Platt 119)
England win after extra time

England: Shilton, Parker, Pearce, Walker, Butcher, Wright,
Waddle, McMahon (Platt, 71), Gascoigne,
Barnes (Bull, 74), Lineker.

QUARTER-FINAL

NAPLES, 1 JULY 1990, 55,205

England (1) 3   **v**   **Cameroon (0) 2**
(Platt 25, Lineker pen 83,   (Kunde pen 61, Ekeke 65)
pen 105)
England win after extra time

England: Shilton, Parker, Pearce, Walker, Butcher (Steven, 73),
Wright, Waddle, Platt, Gascoigne,
Barnes (Beardsley, 46), Lineker.

SEMI-FINAL

TURIN, 4 JULY 1990, 62,628

England (0) 1   **v**   **Germany (0) 1**
(Lineker 80)   (Brehme 60)
Germany won 4–3 on penalties after extra time

England: Shilton, Parker, Pearce, Walker, Butcher (Steven, 70),
Wright, Waddle, Platt, Gascoigne,
Beardsley, Lineker.

Did You Know That?
FIFA permitted England to replace David Seaman in the squad when
the Arsenal goalkeeper injured his thumb in training shortly after
the squad arrived in Italy.

THIRD PLACE PLAY-OFF
BARI, 7 JULY 1990, 51,426

Italy (0) 2   **v**   **England** (0) 1
(Baggio 71,   (Platt 8)
Schillaci pen 86)

England: Shilton, Parker, Dorigo, Stevens, Walker,
Wright (Webb, 71), Steven, McMahon (Wright, 71), Platt,
Beardsley, Lineker.

England's 1990 World Cup Finals Squad

1	Peter Shilton	*(Derby County)*	13	Chris Woods	*(Rangers)*
2	Gary Stevens	*(Rangers)*	14	Mark Wright	*(Derby County)*
3	Stuart Pearce	*(Nottm Forest)*	15	Tony Dorigo	*(Chelsea)*
4	Neil Webb	*(Man Utd)*	16	Steve McMahon	*(Liverpool)*
5	Des Walker	*(Nottm Forest)*	17	David Platt	*(Aston Villa)*
6	Terry Butcher	*(Rangers)*	18	Steve Hodge	*(Nottm Forest)*
7	Bryan Robson	*(Man Utd)*	19	Paul Gascoigne	*(Spurs)*
8	Chris Waddle	*(Marseille)*	20	Trevor Steven	*(Rangers)*
9	Peter Beardsley	*(Liverpool)*	21	Steve Bull	*(Wolves)*
10	Gary Lineker	*(Spurs)*	22	David Seaman	*(Arsenal)*
11	John Barnes	*(Liverpool)*		David Beasant[†]	*(Chelsea)*
12	Paul Parker	*(QPR)*			

Manager: Bobby Robson   *[†]See Did You Know That? on page 105.*

∼ ENGLAND'S FIRST FOOTBALL KNIGHT ∼

John Charles Clegg played in England's first official international
against Scotland at Hampden Park on 30 November 1872, his
only cap. Known as "the Great Old Man of Football", Clegg served
the Football Association for over 51 years. He played for The
Wednesday and Sheffield FC, and later became a director of Sheffield
Wednesday. He also refereed international matches, as well as two
FA Cup Finals. In 1923, aged 73, he was appointed President of the
Football Association and four years later he became the first England
international to be knighted for his services to the game.

∼ JACKIE MILBURN ∼

"Wor Jackie", as he was known, won 13 England caps, scoring nine
times for his country, including a hat-trick against Wales. Jackie was
a Newcastle United legend. He made 492 appearances for United,
scoring 238 times. He died on 8 October 1988, aged 64.

⚜ NINE BLACK PLAYERS ⚜

When England played Australia at West Ham United's Boleyn Ground on 12 February 2003, they used a record nine black players. Sol Campbell, Ashley Cole, Kieron Dyer, Rio Ferdinand and David James all started the game, and all were substituted at half-time. Wes Brown, Jermaine Jenas, Ledley King and Darius Vassell were all used as second-half substitutes. In all, England used 22 players in the game and lost 3–1.

When England played the USA in Chicago on 28 May 2005, David James, Glen Johnson, Ashley Cole, Wes Brown, Sol Campbell, Jermaine Jenas and Kieran Richardson all started the game, and Jermaine Defoe (for Ashley Cole) and Zat Knight (for Sol Campbell) came on as second-half substitutes. Therefore, of the 15 players used in the game by England, nine were black, which is England's highest ever ratio of black players used in a game – 60%. England won 2–1 with both goals from Kieran Richardson.

⚜ CHESTERFIELD SCOTTISH ⚜

Robert "Bob" Primrose Wilson, the Arsenal goalkeeper, appeared twice in 1971 for Scotland's senior team, for which he was eligible through his family ancestry despite the fact that he was born in Chesterfield, England. But he never played against England. Eligibility for the England Schoolboys team depends entirely on the player's place of residence, and players who have appeared for a national schoolboys side in the UK remain free to play for another senior national team.

⚜ DRAGON ALMOST A LION ⚜

Ryan Joseph Giggs was born in Cardiff and therefore was not eligible to play for England's senior side. However, he did play for the England Schoolboys team.

⚜ SALT 'N' LINEKER ⚜

Two former England managers, Sir Bobby Robson and Terry Venables, played an Angel and the Devil respectively in a television advertisement for Walker's crisps in 2004. Sir Bobby was dressed in all-white, and Terry in all-red, as the pair of them represented the opposing sides of Gary Lineker's conscience, offering conflicting advice on various moral dilemmas.

✥

⚜ ENGLAND'S LAST 10 NOTTS MAGPIES ⚜

Player	Years
William Gunn	1884
John Dixon	1885
Charles Dobson	1886
Alfred Shelton	1889–92
Henry Daft	1889–92
George Toone	1892
Percy Humphreys	1903
Herbert Morley	1910
William Ashurst	1923–25
Tommy Lawton	1947–48

Did You Know That?

Notts County are one of the oldest football clubs in the world, formed in November 1862, and have provided players for England's national team since 1883. Three County players, Stuart Macrae, Arthur Cursham and Henry Cursham, played for England against Wales in the 5–0 win at the Kennington Oval on 3 February 1883. Notts County were a Football League Third Division side when Tommy Lawton signed for them, and then played for England. A total of 20 Notts County players have been capped by England.

⚜ SUPER TRAINER ⚜

Les Cocker was the trainer of the 1966 England World Cup winning squad.

⚜ HAT-TRICK OF HAT-TRICKS ⚜

Bobby Charlton scored his third hat-trick for England in their 8–0 whitewash of Mexico at Wembley on 10 May 1961.

⚜ A NEW FORMATION ⚜

Having lost seven of their previous eight internationals against Scotland, conceding 36 goals, the England team arrived for their annual fixture with the "Auld Enemy" at Cathkin Park in 1884 with a new formation. England opted for three half-backs and five forwards as opposed to the customary two half-backs and six forwards. However, Scotland still won 1–0 to record their fifth successive win over England.

✧ THE LIONS ROAR (13) ✧

"David Beckham's sending-off cost us dearly. It was a mistake. But these things happen in football. I am not denying it cost us the game."
Glenn Hoddle finds a convenient scapegoat for England's defeat by Argentina in the 1998 World Cup finals.

✧ ENGLAND SHIRT MAKERS ✧

Two companies have made the England football team shirt:

Admiral ✧ Umbro

✧ VIRTUAL SPECTATOR ✧

When England beat Malta 5–0 at Wembley on 12 May 1971, Gordon Banks only touched the ball four times, all from back passes, and during the 90 minutes didn't have a single save to make.

✧ 14 FROM 8 FOR HILSDON ✧

George Hilsdon won eight caps between 16 February 1907 and 13 February 1909, scoring 14 times for England in the process.

✧ BRITISH ATTENDANCE RECORD SET ✧

On 4 April 1908 a British record crowd of 121,452 fans poured into Hampden Park to see England and Scotland play out a 1–1 draw. The previous record was 110,820 for the 1901 FA Cup Final between Sheffield United and Tottenham Hotspur at the Crystal Palace.

✧ SCOTTISH ENGLISH ✧

Tommy Usher Pearson, who was born in Edinburgh, played at outside-left for England in the 2–1 victory against Scotland in the 1939 unofficial wartime international, played at St James's Park, Newcastle. He also played at outside-left for Scotland in two official 1947 matches, including a 1–1 draw against England.[†]

[†] *Eric Brook and Sam Barkas, both of Manchester City, were the original selections at outside-left and right-back for England in the international at Newcastle, but they were both injured in a car accident on the way to the game and were replaced by two Newcastle United players, Pearson and Joe Richardson.*

✛

∼◦ PETER SHILTON, MBE, OBE ◦∼

Peter Leslie Shilton was born in Leicester on 18 September 1949. Peter's place in England's football history is assured as his country's record cap holder. On 25 November 1970, he made the first of his 125 appearances when England beat East Germany 3–1 at Wembley. Twenty years later Peter made his final appearance for England when they lost 2–1 to Italy in Bari, Italy, in a third place World Cup play-off game at the 1990 finals. If it had not been for Ray Clemence (Liverpool and Tottenham Hotspur), Peter could have exceeded 150 caps as Ray won 61 caps between 1975 and 1981.

Peter signed for Leicester City in September 1966 and when he made his first team appearance aged 16, he was so impressive that Leicester sold their England goalkeeper, Gordon Banks, to Stoke City. Peter was the Foxes' youngest ever debutant and he went on to make 286 appearances for his hometown club, actually scoring once. In 1969, aged 19, Peter made his only appearance in the FA Cup final, when Leicester City lost out to Manchester City.

In November 1974, Peter joined Stoke City setting a new world record fee for a goalkeeper of £325,000. When he left the Victoria Ground he joined Brian Clough's Nottingham Forest in 1977 where he won the First Division Championship in 1978, and two European Cups in 1979 and 1980. After Forest, Peter had spells at Derby County, Plymouth Argyle, Wimbledon, Bolton Wanderers, Coventry City, West Ham United, Leyton Orient and Middlesbrough.

During the 1982 World Cup finals in Spain, Peter conceded just one goal as England remained unbeaten in their five games. He also represented England at the 1986 World Cup finals in Mexico, suffering the infamous "Hand of God" goal and played his last England game at the 1990 Finals in Italy. In his record 125 international appearances for England, he conceded 83 goals, keeping 65 clean sheets, at 0.66 goals per game.

It was at Leyton Orient that Peter became the first, and to date, only English player to make 1,000 Football League appearances. His 1,000th League game was played at Brisbane Road in December 1996, keeping a clean sheet as Leyton Orient beat Brighton & Hove Albion 2–0. When he retired, Peter had played 1,005 Football League games.

Did You Know That?
Peter Shilton was the last player born in the 1940s to play League football in England.

TWO GAMES, TWO GOALS, 1 MINUTE

Tommy Lawton of Chelsea scored goals for England in less than a minute in consecutive internationals. On 27 May 1947 he scored against Portugal in Lisbon after just 17 seconds, and in his next international, on 21 September 1947, he scored after just 34 seconds against Belgium in Brussels.

BRITISH CHAMPIONS

England won the British Home International Championships for the first time in 1888 with a resounding 5–1 win over Scotland, having already beaten both Ireland and Wales 5–1.

THE FIRST GAME ON FOREIGN SOIL

England played their first game on foreign soil when they beat Austria 6–1 in Vienna on 6 June 1908. George Hilsdon (2), James Windridge (2), Arthur Bridgett and Vivian Woodward all scored for England.

ENGLAND WIN OLYMPIC GOLD

The United Kingdom, represented by an England side chosen by the FA, beat Denmark 2–0 at the White City Stadium in the 1908 London Olympics Football Final.

FIRST EVER DOUBLE DOUBLE HAT-TRICK

Vivian Woodward, Tottenham Hotspur's and England's prolific goalscorer, became the first player to score a double hat-trick in two games. He scored six times for England against Holland in an amateur international at Stamford Bridge on 11 December 1909, having already netted eight times against the French three years earlier.

TALKING TACTICS

On 4 April 1930, the England players met up for the first time on the Friday before an international to discuss tactics. The team talk paid off as England beat Scotland 5–2 at Wembley the next day. The win guaranteed England the 1930 British Home International Championship and was also their best win over the "Auld Enemy" since 1893, when they won by the same score.

⚜

⟋ EUROPEAN CHAMPIONSHIP 1992 ⟋

In 1992 England participated in their fourth European Championship finals, which were held in Sweden. At the finals, England were drawn in Group 1 with Denmark, France and the hosts, Sweden. England drew their opening two games 0–0 with Denmark and France in Malmö Stadion, and lost their final group game 2–1 to their hosts, Sweden in the Råsunda Stadion, Solna, a result that left England bottom of the group with just two points.

The surprise winners of the tournament were Denmark, last-minute replacements for the suspended Yugoslavia. They arrived with little time to prepare, and walked off with the trophy after beating Germany 2–0 in the Final in Gothenburg.

FIRST ROUND, GROUP 1

11 JUNE 1992, MALMO, 26,400

Denmark (0) **0**   v   **England** (0) **0**

England: Woods, Steven, Pearce, Curle (Daley, 62), Keown, Walker, Palmer, Platt, Merson (Webb, 71), Lineker, Smith.

---

14 JUNE 1992, MALMO, 26,500

France (0) **0**   v   **England** (0) **0**

England: Woods, Sinton, Pearce, Walker, Keown, Steven, Batty, Palmer, Platt, Shearer, Lineker.

---

17 JUNE 1992, STOCKHOLM, 30,100

Sweden (0) **2**   v   **England** (1) **1**
(Eriksson 54, Brolin 83)   (Platt 5)

England: Woods, Sinton (Merson, 77), Pearce, Keown, Walker, Batty, Webb, Palmer, Platt, Daley, Lineker (Smith 65).

Group 1 – Final table

	P	W	D	L	F	A	Pts
Sweden	3	2	1	0	4	2	5
Denmark	3	1	1	1	2	2	3
France	3	0	2	1	2	3	2
England	3	0	2	1	1	2	2

England's 1992 European Championship Finals Squad

1	Chris Woods *(Sheffield Wed)*	13	Nigel Martyn *(Crystal Palace)*
2	Keith Curle *(Man City)*	14	Tony Dorigo *(Leeds United)*
3	Stuart Pearce *(Nottm Forest)*	15	Neil Webb *(Man Utd)*
4	Martin Keown *(Everton)*	16	Paul Merson *(Arsenal)*
5	Des Walker *(Nottm Forest)*	17	Alan Smith *(Arsenal)*
6	Mark Wright *(Liverpool)*	18	Tony Daley *(Aston Villa)*
7	David Platt *(Bari)*	19	David Batty *(Leeds Utd)*
8	Trevor Steven *(Marseille)*	20	Alan Shearer *(Southampton)*
9	Nigel Clough *(Nottm Forest)*		John Barnes *(Liverpool)*, Lee Dixon
10	Gary Lineker *(Spurs)*		*(Arsenal)* and Gary Stevens *(Rangers)*
11	Andy Sinton *(QPR)*		withdrew from the squad because of
12	Carlton Palmer *(Sheffield Wed)*		injuries.

Manager: Graham Taylor

Did You Know That?

It was during the Sweden defeat that the England manager, Graham Taylor, uttered the famous words "Do I not like that" just before Tomas Brolin scored for Sweden.

DIXIE'S 60

William "Dixie" Dean scored twice for England in his debut against Wales on 12 February 1927, then scored another two in his next international, England's 2–1 win over Scotland at Hampden Park on 2 April 1927. It was England's first win on Scottish soil since 1904. The following season, 1927–28, Dixie scored a record 60 League goals to help Everton lift the First Division Championship.

ENGLAND'S NEW AERIAL THREAT

When Newcastle United's wing-half, Samuel Weaver, made his England debut in the 3–0 win over Scotland at Hampden Park on 9 April 1932, he added a new aerial threat to the England attack with his 30-yard throw-ins.

CAUGHT OUT IN THE CORNER

England lost 1–0 to Scotland at Hampden Park on 13 April 1929. The game was heading for a 0–0 draw when remarkably, with only minutes remaining, Alex Cheyne scored direct from a corner against John Hacking of Oldham Athletic in the England goal. It was the first time a player had scored direct from a corner in an international.

⚜

ENGLAND'S LAST 10 BRUMMIE BLUES

Player	Years
Lewis Stoker	1932–34
Arthur Grosvenor	1933
Gil Merrick	1951–54
Jeffrey Hall	1955–57
Gordon Astall	1956
Trevor Smith	1959
Mike Hellawell	1962
Trevor Francis	1977–78
Matthew Upson	2003–04
Emile Heskey	2004

Did You Know That?

Two Birmingham City players started for England for the first time on 5 April 1930 when goalkeeper Harry Hibbs and Joe Bradford played against Scotland. A total of 16 Birmingham City players have been capped by England up to the end of 2005.

THE BOGOTA BRACELET

On the 18 May 1970 the England team were in the Tequendama Hotel in Bogota, preparing to face Colombia later that day in a warm-up match prior to the World Cup finals in Mexico. Bobby Charlton and Bobby Moore were in The Green Fire jewellery shop, situated in the hotel's foyer, looking for a present for Bobby Charlton's wife. They left the shop and sat on some seats in the foyer only a few yards from the jewellery shop. Within minutes Clara Padilla, an assistant from the shop, accused Bobby Moore of stealing an emerald and diamond bracelet. As it turned out there was no truth in the accusation, but it was not until five years later that Bobby finally received a letter from the Foreign Office telling him that the case was closed.

CAMPBELL INJURY SAVES UTD RECORD

Rio Ferdinand, who had been dropped for England's game against Austria on 8 October 2005 in favour of Sol Campbell, came on as a second-half substitute for the Arsenal defender. Had Ferdinand not come on it would have been the first time since the Euro 96 semi-final defeat to Germany that an England team did not field a Manchester United player.

⚜ BANKS OF ENGLAND ⚜

During his career Gordon Banks played for Chesterfield, Leicester City, Stoke City and the Fort Lauderdale Strikers. He made 73 appearances for England, keeping a clean sheet in 35 of the games. After the 1970 World Cup finals the legendary Pele said of Banks: "For me, Banks was the leading goalkeeper of the 1970 games, and quite possibly the leading defender in any position."

In addition to the 1966 World Cup, Gordon won the Football League Cup with Leicester City in 1964 and again with Stoke City in 1972. Gordon is England's second most capped goalkeeper behind Peter Shilton. Gordon's career was ended in 1974 after he suffered an eye injury in a car crash.

⚜ MR RELIABLE BETWEEN THE POSTS ⚜

Gordon Banks has the best "goals against" average in World Cup finals for his country, with 0.43 goals conceded per 90 minutes played in nine games at the 1966 and 1970 finals. Peter Shilton is second with 0.56 in 17 games at the 1982, 1986 and 1990 finals.

⚜ A SAFE PAIR OF HANDS ⚜

Peter Shilton conceded only one goal in five games at the finals of the World Cup in Spain in 1982, the fewest goals conceded by an England goalkeeper during a World Cup tournament.

⚜ THE BOBBY MOORE BRIDGE ⚜

The Bobby Moore Bridge is situated beside the old Wembley Stadium. There is a plaque on the bridge in tribute to England's 1966 World Cup winning captain that reads "In honour of a football legend".

⚜ THREE-WAY SPLIT ⚜

The British Home International Championships went to a three-way split in 1903 for the first time in its history with England, Ireland and Scotland all level with four points.

⚜ ENGLAND JOIN FIFA ⚜

England joined the Fédération Internationale de Football Association (FIFA) in 1905.

⚜ HEAD-TO-HEAD WITH GERMANY ⚜

	Played	Won	Drawn	Lost	For	Against
WC Finals	4	1	2	1	7	6
ECQ Home	1	0	0	1	1	3
ECQ Away	1	0	1	0	0	0
Friendly Home	4	3	0	1	7	3
Friendly Away	6	3	0	3	9	7
Total	16	7	3	6	24	19

⚜ HEAD-TO-HEAD WITH WEST GERMANY ⚜

	Played	Won	Drawn	Lost	For	Against
WCQ Home	1	0	0	1	0	1
WCQ Away	1	1	0	0	5	1
EC Finals	2	1	1	0	2	1
Friendly Home	2	1	0	1	3	1
Friendly Away	3	1	1	1	10	8
Total	9	4	2	3	20	12

⚜ BILLY AND JOY ⚜

Long before Posh and Becks grabbed all the headlines, England captain Billy Wright married Joy Beverley, a member of the famous Beverley Sisters in 1959. The Beverley Sisters were Britain's and Europe's most successful and highest paid female singing act during the 1950s and 1960s. They broke box-office records wherever they appeared, and had many hit records including *I Saw Mummy Kissing Santa Claus*, *Little Donkey* and *Drummer Boy*. Billy and Joy were together for 36 years.

⚜ AN ABBOTT AND A CHRISTIAN ⚜

Edward Christian won one cap for England against Scotland in England's 5–4 win on 5 April 1879, while Walter Abbott also won one cap, against Wales on 3 March 1902 in a 0–0 draw.

⚜ TON-UP FOR ENGLAND AT WEMBLEY ⚜

On 13 December 1989 England played Yugoslavia in a friendly international at Wembley. England won 2–0, with both goals coming from their captain, Bryan Robson. The win was England's hundredth competitive victory at Wembley Stadium.

ENGLAND'S LAST 10 BLACK CATS

Player	Years
Len Shackleton	1948–54
Willie Watson	1949–50
Colin Grainger	1957
Stan Anderson	1962
Dave Watson	1974–75
Tony Towers	1976
Nick Pickering	1983
Kevin Phillips	1999–2002
Michael Gray	1999
Gavin McCann	2001

Did You Know That?
Three Sunderland players started for England against Ireland in Belfast on 15 February 1913: Charlie Buchan, Francis Cuggy and John Mordue. Buchan scored for England in a 2–1 defeat. A total of 24 Sunderland players have been capped by England.

THE LIONS ROAR (14)

"That man could talk and talk and talk until the cows came home and he'd continue talking until they were fast asleep. The problem was most of it didn't make any sense to me."
Ian Wright on Graham Taylor's England team talks.

29 GOALS IN 23 INTERNATIONALS

Vivian Woodward[†] scored 29 goals for England in 23 internationals, including four in England's 8–2 win over Hungary in Budapest on 31 May 1909.

8,600 FEET AND FOUR GOALS

In a warm-up game for the 1970 World Cup finals, England beat Colombia 4–0 in Bogota on 20 May 1970. The venue, at an altitude of 8,600 feet, was chosen to help acclimatize the England players to the thin air of Mexico. Martin Peters scored twice with Alan Ball and Bobby Charlton scoring the other two.

†The day after Woodward scored four against Hungary, he scored a hat-trick in England's 8–1 win over Austria in Vienna.

ENGLAND XI – SHEFFIELD WEDNESDAY

1
Chris
WOODS

2
Mel
STERLAND

6
Des
WALKER

5
Peter
SWAN

3
Andy
HINCHCLIFFE

7
Chris
WADDLE

8
Jackie
SEWELL

4
Carlton
PALMER

11
Albert
QUIXALL

9
David
HIRST

10
Fred
SPIKSLEY

Substitutes
Ron *SPRINGETT*, John *FATHAM*, John *ROBINSON*,
Gerry *YOUNG*, Ronnie *STARLING*
Manager
Howard *WILKINSON*

Did You Know That?
The club was formed on 4 September 1867 and was, in the beginning, a cricket team, with football being played during the winter to keep the team together. Sheffield Wednesday turned professional in 1887 and were elected to the First Division of the Football League in 1892.

WEMBLEY'S SECOND VISITORS

On 9 May 1951, Argentina became the second national team to play England at Wembley in an official international match. England won 2–1 thanks to two goals from Blackpool's Stan Mortensen.

FIRST DEFEAT ON ENGLISH SOIL

On 21 September 1949 the Republic of Ireland beat England 2–0 at Goodison Park, Liverpool, thus becoming the first foreign team to beat England on English soil.

⚜ PFA PLAYERS' PLAYER OF THE YEAR ⚜

The Professional Football Association's Players' Player of the Year was introduced in 1974. The award goes to the player who, in the opinion of his fellow professionals, was the outstanding English League player of the season. Since its inception, 15 England internationals have won the award 16 times, with Alan Shearer winning it twice.

1974	– Norman Hunter	Leeds Utd
1975	– Colin Todd	Derby County
1978	– Peter Shilton	Nottingham Forest
1980	– Terry McDermott	Liverpool
1982	– Kevin Keegan	Southampton
1985	– Peter Reid	Everton
1986	– Gary Lineker	Everton
1987	– Clive Allen	Tottenham Hotspur
1988	– John Barnes	Liverpool
1990	– David Platt	Aston Villa
1992	– Gary Pallister	Manchester United
1995	– Alan Shearer	Blackburn Rovers
1996	– Les Ferdinand	Newcastle United
1997	– Alan Shearer	Newcastle United
2001	– Teddy Sheringham	Manchester United
2005	– John Terry	Chelsea

⚜ HOMESICK GOALKEEPER ⚜

Everton goalkeeper Gordon West, who had already won three international caps with England, informed Sir Alf Ramsey on 9 August 1969 that he did not wish to be considered for the England squad for the 1970 World Cup finals in Mexico. West told Sir Alf that he would be homesick. He was never picked again to play for England.

⚜ AFTER YOU BRO! ⚜

On 22 April 1998 Phil Neville replaced his brother, Gary, against Portugal at Wembley. This was the only occasion in which an England player was substituted by his brother.

⚜ ENGLAND'S ONE AND ONLY STROLLER ⚜

Alf Harvey of Wednesbury Strollers played against Wales in 1881.

In 1996, England were the host nation for the European Championship finals. England were in Group A with Holland, Switzerland and Scotland. In their opening game, England could only manage a 1–1 draw with the Swiss. In their next game England beat Scotland 2–0 at Wembley. Holland were England's next opponents and two goals each from Alan Shearer and Teddy Sheringham gave England an impressive 4–1 victory. England topped the group and met Spain in the quarter-finals in a game that went to extra-time (0–0) and had to be settled on penalties. England won the penalty shoot-out 4–2 to progress to the semi-finals and a match against Germany. Just as their quarter-final match went to extra-time, so did England's semi-final (1–1), and then on to penalties which England lost 6–5.

Germany went on to beat the Czech Republic 2–1 in the Final at Wembley, with two goals by Oliver Bierhoff replying to Patrik Berger's 58th minute penalty for the Czechs.

FIRST ROUND, GROUP A
8 JUNE 1996, WEMBLEY, 76,567
England (1) 1   v   **Switzerland** (0) 1
(Shearer 23)   (Turkylmaz 84)

England: Seaman, Neville, G., Pearce, Adams, Southgate, Anderton, Gascoigne (Platt, 77), McManaman (Stone, 67), Sheringham (Barmby, 67), Shearer.

---

15 JUNE 1996, WEMBLEY, 77,000
England (1) 2   v   **Scotland** (0) 0
(Shearer 53, Gascoigne 79)

England: Seaman, Neville, G., Pearce (Redknapp, 46 [Campbell, 85]) Adams, Southgate, Ince (Stone, 80), Anderton, Gascoigne, McManaman, Sheringham, Shearer.

---

18 JUNE 1996, WEMBLEY, 76,798
England (1) 4   v   **Holland** (0) 1
(Shearer 23, 57,   (Kluivert 78)
Sheringham 51, 62)

England: Seaman, Neville, G., Pearce, Adams, Southgate, Ince (Platt, 67), McManaman, Gascoigne, Anderton, Sheringham (Fowler, 75), Shearer (Barmby, 75).

Group A – Final table

	P	W	D	L	F	A	Pts
England	3	2	1	0	7	2	7
Holland	3	1	1	1	3	4	4
Scotland	3	1	1	1	1	2	4
Switzerland	3	0	1	2	1	4	1

QUARTER-FINAL
22 JUNE 1996, WEMBLEY, 75,440

England (0) 0   v   Spain (0) 0
England won 4–2 on penalties after extra time

England: Seaman, Neville, G., Pearce, Adams, Southgate,
McManaman (Stone, 109), Platt, Gascoigne, Anderton (Barmby, 109),
Sheringham (Fowler, 109), Shearer.

SEMI-FINAL
26 JUNE 1996, WEMBLEY, 75,862

England (1) 1   v   Germany (1) 1
(Shearer 3)   (Kuntz 16)
Germany won 6–5 on penalties after extra time

England: Seaman, Ince, Pearce, Adams, Southgate,
McManaman, Platt, Gascoigne, Anderton,
Sheringham, Shearer.

England's Euro 96 Finals Squad

1	David Seaman	*(Arsenal)*	12	Steve Howey	*(Newcastle Utd)*
2	Gary Neville	*(Man Utd)*	13	Tim Flowers	*(Blackburn)*
3	Stuart Pearce	*(Nottm Forest)*	14	Nicky Barmby	*(Middlesbrough)*
4	Paul Ince	*(Inter Milan)*	15	Jamie Redknapp	*(Liverpool)*
5	Tony Adams	*(Arsenal)*	16	Sol Campbell	*(Spurs)*
6	Gareth Southgate	*(Aston Villa)*	17	Steve McManaman	*(Liverpool)*
7	David Platt	*(Arsenal)*	18	Les Ferdinand	*(Newcastle Utd)*
8	Paul Gascoigne	*(Rangers)*	19	Philip Neville	*(Man Utd)*
9	Alan Shearer	*(Blackburn)*	20	Steve Stone	*(Nottm Forest)*
10	Teddy Sheringham	*(Spurs)*	21	Robbie Fowler	*(Liverpool)*
11	Darren Anderton	*(Spurs)*	22	Ian Walker	*(Spurs)*

Manager: Terry Venables

Did You Know That?

The semi-final defeat against Germany was England's 13th game of the
1995–96 season, and the only contest they lost during that period.

⟶ NAT LOFTHOUSE, OBE ⟵

Nathaniel Lofthouse was born on 27 August 1925 and played for Bolton Wanderers for his entire professional career. He signed for Bolton as an apprentice on 4 September 1939, and made his debut against Bury on 22 March 1941, scoring twice in a 5–1 win. However, it was a further five years before he made his league debut for the club, in a game against Chelsea on 31 August 1946, again scoring twice but this time in a 4–3 defeat.

Nat made his England debut on 22 November 1950, the first of 33 caps he won for his country, in a game against Yugoslavia at Arsenal Stadium. Amazingly, Nat scored both England goals in a 2–2 draw. On 25 May 1952, Nat was nicknamed "The Lion of Vienna" by the press after he scored twice in England's 3–2 win over Austria in the Prater Stadium, Vienna. People couldn't believe he put his personal safety to one side, after being knocked out cold by the Austrian goalkeeper as he raced in on goal to score England's winner.

During the 1952–53 season Nat became one of only 12 players to score in every round of the FA Cup, including the Final. However, Bolton lost the Final, later dubbed "The Matthews Final", to a Stanley Matthews inspired Blackpool side that beat Bolton 4–3 at Wembley. However, Nat finally got his hands on the trophy when he captained Bolton to victory over a depleted Manchester United side in the 1958 FA Cup Final. United reached the 1958 Final despite eight of their players losing their lives in the Munich air disaster on 6 February 1958. Nat scored both goals for Bolton in their 2–0 win at Wembley.

In 1953, he was named the English Footballer of the Year after topping the First Division goalscoring charts with 30 goals. On 20 May 1956, Nat broke Steve Bloomer's 49-year-old England goalscoring record by netting his 29th internatioanl goal after coming on as a substitute for Tommy Taylor (Manchester United) in a 5–1 win against Finland in Helsinki (he scored twice in the game). On 22 October 1958, Nat made his final appearance for England, against the USSR, aged 33, and fittingly scored in England's 5–0 win under the Twin Towers. In January 1960, Nat announced that he was retiring as a result of an ankle injury and, on 17 December 1960, he made his final league appearance for his beloved Bolton Wanderers. He created a club goalscoring record of 285 goals in 503 appearances for Bolton (256 goals in 452 league matches, a remarkable goal average of better than one goal every two games). In 1986, he became Bolton Wanderers' club president.

⚓ ENGLAND'S 10 COTTAGERS ⚓

Player	Years
Frank Osborne	1922–23
Leonard Oliver	1929
Albert Barrett	1929
John Arnold	1933
James Taylor	1951
Bedford Jezzard	1954–55
Johnny Haynes	1954–62
Ernie Langley	1958
George Cohen	1964–67
Zat Knight	2005

Did You Know That?
Only on four occasions have two Fulham players appeared in the same England team. This most recently occurred when Ernie Langley and Johnny Haynes played together in the 5–0 defeat to Yugoslavia in Belgrade on 11 May 1958.

⚓ BALL BOUNCED OUT ⚓

On 20 August 1975 Gerry Francis of Queen's Park Rangers was appointed the new captain of England. The previous captain, World Cup winner Alan Ball, was not even named in the England squad to face Switzerland in a friendly in Basle on 3 September 1975.

⚓ COURTING SIR ALF ⚓

In January 1970 Sir Alf Ramsey was approached by Portuguese giants Benfica and asked to name his price to manage the team. Sir Alf turned them down to concentrate on trying to retain the World Cup with England at Mexico in 1970.

⚓ ENGLAND'S NEWCASTLE MANAGERS ⚓

Charlie Mitten (1958 – 1961) ❖ William McGarry (1977 – 1980)
Jack Charlton (1984 – 1985) ❖ Kevin Keegan (1992 – 1997)
Sir Bobby Robson (1999 – 2004)

⚓ PILGRIM'S PROGRESS ⚓

Harry Swepstone of the Pilgrims won six England caps (1880–83).

⟶ ON TARGET AGAINST WALES ⟵

The last 10 England players to score against Wales are:

Joe Cole	Millennium Stadium	3 September 2005
David Beckham	Old Trafford	9 October 2004
Frank Lampard Jnr	Old Trafford	9 October 2004
Phil Neal	Wembley	23 February 1983
Terry Butcher	Wembley	23 February 1983
Trevor Francis	Ninian Park, Cardiff	27 April 1982
Paul Mariner	Wrexham	17 May 1980
Peter Barnes	Ninian Park, Cardiff	13 May 1978
Tony Currie	Ninian Park, Cardiff	13 May 1978
Bob Latchford	Ninian Park, Cardiff	13 May 1978

⟶ FIRST 0–0 IN ALMOST 100 YEARS ⟵

When England drew 0–0 with Scotland at Hampden Park in the British Home International Championships on 25 April 1970, it was the first time they had played out a scoreless draw since their first ever official meeting in 1872.

⟶ WORLD CUP WINNING TRIO LEFT OUT ⟵

When the England squad for their international against East Germany was announced on 16 November 1970, both Charlton brothers and Gordon Banks were left out of the squad. Peter Shilton of Leicester City made his debut in England's 3–1 win nine days later.

⟶ THE CRYING GAME ⟵

Paul Gascoigne is famous for his "crying incident" during England's World Cup semi-final with Germany at Italia '90. He later made fun of himself by appearing in a television advertisement for Walker's Crisps in which he burst into tears after Gary Lineker stopped him stealing his crisps.

⟶ KEEGAN QUITS ⟵

Following England's 1–0 defeat to Germany in the last ever game to be played at the old Wembley Stadium, England boss Kevin Keegan stunned a post-match news conference by announcing he was quitting his position as national team manager.

✠

⚔ FA ANGERS GERMANY ⚔

Bert Millichip, the FA Chairman, was alleged to have reneged on a handshake deal with Germany over the 2006 World Cup finals. After England hosted Euro 96, Millichip reportedly agreed to back Germany as hosts for the 2006 World Cup finals, but a few months later the FA submitted a rival bid for the finals, much to the anger of the Germans.

⚔ REVIE WALKS OUT ON ENGLAND ⚔

In 1977 England manager Don Revie walked out on the national team to take a highly paid, tax-free job in the United Arab Emirates. Revie negotiated the deal in Dubai instead of watching an international in Finland.

⚔ TURNIP HEAD ⚔

Graham Taylor's England failed to win a single game at the 1992 European Championship, and also failed to qualify for the 1994 World Cup finals in the USA. Following Sweden's 2–1 win over England during the 1992 European Championship, *The Sun* newspaper superimposed Taylor's head on a photograph of a turnip with the headline: Swedes 2 Turnips 1.

⚔ ENGLAND'S BOLTON MANAGERS ⚔

Nat Lofthouse (1968–1970) ❖ Jimmy Meadows (1971)
Jimmy Armfield (1971–1974) ❖ Stan Anderson (1980–1981)
Phil Neal (1985–1992) ❖ Roy McFarland & Colin Todd (1995–1996)
Colin Todd (1996–1999)

⚔ FIRST HOME WORLD CUP QUALIFIER ⚔

England played their first home World Cup qualifying game at Maine Road on 16 November 1949, beating Northern Ireland 9–2. Jack Rowley scored four goals.

⚔ 42 IN 42 FOR LINEKER ⚔

Gary Lineker of Tottenham Hotspur scored his 42nd goal for England in the 42nd second of England's 4–1 win against Malaysia in Kuala Lumpa on 12 June 1991. Lineker scored all four England goals.

⚯ ENGLAND'S LAST 10 POMPEY BOYS ⚯

Player	Years
Albert Houlker	1903
Arthur Knight	1919
John Smith	1931
Jimmy Allen	1933
Freddie Worrall	1935–36
Jimmy Dickinson	1949–56
Peter Harris	1949–54
Jack Froggatt	1949–53
Len Phillips	1951–54
Mark Hateley	1984

Did You Know That?
Two Pompey players started for England on several occasions throughout the late 1940s and early 1950s. The first time this occurred was when Jimmy Dickinson and Peter Harris played in England's 2–0 home defeat to Eire on 21 September 1949, England's first defeat to a foreign team on English soil. Jimmy Dickinson started alongside Jack Froggatt 12 times between 1949 and 1953. A total of 11 Portsmouth players have been capped by England.

⚯ THE LIONS ROAR (15) ⚯

"I just feel I fall a little short of what is required in this job. I sat there in the first half and could see things weren't going right but I couldn't find it in myself to solve the problem."
Kevin Keegan announcing his resignation as manager after England's exit from Euro 2000.

⚯ FIRST LOSS AT HOME IN A WCQ ⚯

Having played their first World Cup qualifying game in 1949, it was not until 12 February 1997 that England lost their first home World Cup qualifying game when Italy won 1–0 at Wembley.

⚯ TWO GOALS PER GAME ⚯

George Camsell, who won nine caps between 9 May 1929 and 9 May 1936, scored in every game he played for England. Indeed, Camsell scored a total of 18 goals for his country, an average of two goals per game.

✧ DIDN'T LAST THE PACE ✧

Bryan Robson was substituted four times during his World Cup career for England, in the group match against Czechoslovakia in 1982, in group matches against Portugal and Morocco in 1986 and, finally, in the group match against Holland at Italia '90. Robson was injured each time.

✧ THE FIRST BLACK ENGLAND PLAYER ✧

Viv Anderson became England's first black player when he made his debut against Czechoslovakia at Wembley on 29 November 1978.

✧ VICTORY INTERNATIONALS ✧

England played Scotland twice at the end of the 1918–19 season in unofficial "Victory" internationals. The two sides drew 2–2 at Goodison Park and England won 4–3 at Hampden Park.

✧ ENGLISHMAN HELPS SPAIN ✧

England lost abroad for the first time when Spain beat them 4–3 in Madrid on 15 May 1929. The Spanish team was coached by the former Middlesbrough and England international winger, Frederick Pentland.

✧ FIRST HOME EURO QUALIFIER ✧

England played their first home European Championships qualifying game at Hillsborough, Sheffield, on 3 October 1962. Ron Flowers of Wolverhampton Wanderers scored for England in a 1–1 draw with France.

✧ FIRST AWAY EURO QUALIFIER ✧

England played their first away European Championships qualifying game in Paris on 27 February 1963. Bobby Smith of Spurs and Bobby Tambling of Chelsea scored for England in a 5–2 defeat to France.

✧ MAINE ROAD MASSACRE ✧

England thrashed Scotland 8–0 at Maine Road on 16 October 1945. Everton's Tommy Lawton scored four times, including a first-half hat-trick in only 10 minutes.

⚔ WORLD CUP FINALS – FRANCE 1998 ⚔

France hosted the 1998 World Cup finals between 10 June and 12 July. England got off to a good start with a 2–0 win over Tunisia in Marseille on 15 June. A week later England lost 2–1 to Romania in Toulouse, but a 2–0 win over Colombia in Lens was enough to see England through to the next stage of the tournament as group runners-up. In their second phase match England were drawn to face Argentina in a game that provided an opportunity for England to avenge the infamous "Hand of God" goal against them twelve years earlier in Mexico. The game played in Stade Geoffroy-Guichard, Saint-Etienne, was a tense affair and ended 2–2 at the end of 90 minutes. England were down to 10 men after David Beckham, who was lying on the pitch at the time, was sent off for flicking his foot at Diego Simeone. Extra-time was played but no further goals were added. The game had to be decided by a penalty shoot-out which England lost 4–3. France beat Brazil 3–0 in the Final.

FIRST ROUND, GROUP G
MARSEILLE, 15 JUNE 1998, 54,587
England (1) 2   v   **Tunisia** (0) 0
(Shearer 43, Scholes 89)

England: Seaman, Campbell, Le Saux, Southgate, Adams,
Batty, Ince, Scholes, Anderton,
Sheringham (Owen, 85), Shearer.

TOULOUSE, 22 JUNE 1998, 33,500
Romania (0) 2   v   **England** (0) 1
(Moldovan 47, Petrescu 90)   (Owen 79)

England: Seaman, Campbell, Le Saux, Southgate, Adams,
Batty, Ince (Beckham, 32), Scholes, Anderton,
Sheringham (Owen, 72), Shearer.

LENS, 26 JUNE 1998, 38,100
Columbia (0) 0   v   **England** (2) 2
(Anderton 20,
Beckham 29)

England: Seaman, Neville G, Le Saux, Adams, Campbell, Beckham,
Ince (Batty, 83), Scholes (McManaman, 73), Anderton (Lee, 79),
Owen, Shearer.

Group G – Final table

	P	W	D	L	F	A	Pts
Romania	3	2	1	0	4	2	7
England	3	2	0	1	5	2	6
Colombia	3	1	0	2	1	3	4
Tunisia	3	0	1	2	1	4	1

SECOND ROUND
ST ETIENNE, 30 JUNE 1998, 30,600
Argentina (2) 2   v   England (2) 2
(Batistuta pen 6, Zanetti 45)   (Shearer pen 10, Owen 16)
England lost 4–3 on penalties

England: Seaman, Neville G, Le Saux (Southgate, 71), Campbell, Adams, Beckham, Ince, Merson (Scholes, 78), Anderton (Batty, 97), Owen, Shearer.

England's 1998 World Cup Finals Squad

1	David Seaman *(Arsenal)*	12	Gary Neville *(Man Utd)*
2	Sol Campbell *(Spurs)*	13	Nigel Martyn *(Leeds Utd)*
3	Graeme Le Saux *(Chelsea)*	14	Darren Anderton *(Spurs)*
4	Paul Ince *(Liverpool)*	15	Paul Merson *(Arsenal)*
5	Tony Adams *(Arsenal)*	16	Paul Scholes *(Man Utd)*
6	Gareth Southgate *(Aston Villa)*	17	Robert Lee *(Newcastle Utd)*
7	David Beckham *(Man Utd)*	18	Martin Keown *(Arsenal)*
8	David Batty *(Newcastle Utd)*	19	Les Ferdinand *(Spurs)*
9	Alan Shearer *(Newcastle Utd)*	20	Michael Owen *(Liverpool)*
10	Teddy Sheringham *(Man Utd)*	21	Rio Ferdinand *(West Ham)*
11	Steve McManaman *(Liverpool)*	22	Tim Flowers *(Blackburn)*

Manager: Glenn Hoddle

Did You Know That?
Many England fans and journalists blamed David Beckham for England's elimination from the tournament. An effigy of Beckham was hung-up outside a London pub as he became the target of severe criticism and abuse. One newspaper even printed a dartboard with a photograph of Beckham on it.

⟶ NINE GOALS FOR TWO VILLANS ⟵

In England's first match against Ireland on 18 February 1892, Oliver Vaughton and Arthur Brown, both of Aston Villa, scored 5 goals and 4 goals respectively in a 13–0 win.

⚜

⟿ SIR STANLEY MATTHEWS, CBE ⟿

Stanley Matthews was born on 1 January 1915 in Stoke-on-Trent. In 1929, he joined the Stoke City ground staff aged 14 and was paid £1 per week. Just six weeks after he turned 17, Stan made his first-team debut for Stoke. In 1934 he fell out with his manager and asked for a transfer. The transfer request shocked the Stoke fans that much that local businessmen pleaded with the club to settle the dispute because it was affecting morale and production in their factories. However, in 1947, a further fall-out resulted in Stan being sold to Blackpool for £11,500. He was 32 at the time.

On 29 September 1934, Stan made his England debut in a British Home Championship game against Wales in Cardiff. England won 4–0 with Stan scoring. At Blackpool Stan reached three FA Cup finals, losing to Manchester United in 1948 and to Newcastle United in 1951. However, perhaps the greatest moment of his career came in 1953 when Blackpool faced Bolton Wanderers in the FA Cup Final at Wembley. Over half a century later football fans across the world still refer to the 1953 Final as "The Matthews Final". Blackpool were 3–1 down with 20 minutes remaining. Then the "Wizard of the Dribble" took the game by the scruff of the neck and helped Blackpool to a historic 4–3 win in normal time.

On 15 May 1957, Stan wore the England shirt for the 54th and last time in a 4–1 win over Denmark in Copenhagen. He scored nine goals for his country. In 1961, aged 46, Stan returned to his boyhood heroes, Stoke. He cost Stoke £3,500 but it was money well spent because when he pulled on the famous red-and-white striped shirt again the club's average gate rose from 9,000 to a staggering 36,000, such was his appeal. Despite his age Stan inspired Stoke to promotion to the English First Division when he was 48-years old. He never drank, never smoked and he ate salads, getting up every morning before 6.00 a.m. to train. Stan played his last game for Stoke City aged 51 years and 5 days, and is the oldest player to have played a competitive game in English top-flight football, a record that will never be beaten.

On 23 January 2000, Stan died at 85. The people of Stoke turned out to pay homage when his funeral procession passed through the city. Stan's ashes are buried beneath the centre spot at Stoke City's Britannia Stadium. Sir Stanley Matthews, CBE, was the first "Gentleman of Football". Having served with the RAF during World War II, his professional career spanned 34 years. He played almost 700 league games, and was never once cautioned.

⚬ BRING ON THE SCOTS ⚬

England had more wins at Wembley against Scotland, 16 in 30 matches, than against any other country. Against Northern Ireland they had 13 wins in 18 matches, and against Wales 10 wins in 16 matches.

⚬ LUCKY SHIRTS ⚬

England's most successful shirt in terms of the number of actual games won was the 1974 white home shirt manufactured by Admiral, first worn on 30 October 1974. This also marked the start of Don Revie's spell in charge of the national team, which saw England beat Czechoslovakia 3–0 at Wembley in a 1976 European Championship qualifying game. In total England wore the shirt 44 times from 30 October 1974 to 26 March 1980, winning 29 times, with eight draws and only seven losses. However, despite the success of the shirt, it never appeared at a major finals tournament.

⚬ COME ON YOU YELLOWS ⚬

When England played Team America in the 1976 Bicentennial Tournament in the United States they took to the pitch in an all-yellow strip.

⚬ THE MIGHTY MAGYARS ⚬

Hungary humiliated England at Wembley on 25 November 1953, winning 6–3 to become the first foreign team from outside the British Isles to beat England on English soil. This was Hungary's only success over England at Wembley, however, as they lost their other six matches – a higher number of defeats than any other foreign team suffered at the stadium.[†]

⚬ THE WEMBLEY WIZARDS ⚬

Scotland were the first of 17 countries to beat England at Wembley. The first of their nine Wembley wins came in 1928 when the famous "Wembley Wizards" thrashed England 5–1 on 31 March.[††]

[†]In January 2006, the FA announced that England's first opponents at the new Wembley would be Hungary. Unfortunately, delays in completing the stadium meant the game was switched.
[††]England did not gain their first win at the stadium until 1930 when, in their third Wembley international, they beat Scotland 5–2.

Player	Years
Bryan Douglas	1957–63
Keith Newton	1966–69
Alan Shearer	1992–96
Stuart Ripley	1993–97
David Batty	1994–95
Tim Flowers	1994–98
Graeme Le Saux	1994–97
Jason Wilcox	1996–99
Chris Sutton	1997
David Dunn	2002

Did You Know That?
Five Blackburn Rovers players were in England's starting line-up when they beat Ireland 9–1 in Belfast on 15 March 1890: John Barton, James Forrest, Joe Lofthouse, Nat Walton and Bill Townley. Barton, Lofthouse and Townley all scored in the game. A total of 45 Blackburn players have been capped by England.

—∘ FAITH HEALER DROPPED BY THE FA ∘—

Following the sacking of England coach Glenn Hoddle in early 1999, the FA also dropped faith healer Eileen Drewery from the "squad". The FA said players were free to see the former pub landlady but made it clear that they would no longer pay the £25 per visit fees. In response to the actions of the FA, Mrs Drewery said that she was determined to retain her links with England players. "They can't sack me because I have no boss apart from God," said Mrs Drewery.

—∘ MULLET HEADS ∘—

The mullet is a type of haircut, in which the hair is allowed to grow long at the back of the head (usually at least to the shoulders), but cut shorter on the top, front, and sides of the head. The following England players all sported a mullet:

Glenn Hoddle ❖ Paul Mariner ❖ Chris Waddle

—∘ SWEDISH LION ∘—

Sven-Goran Eriksson was the first foreigner to manage England.

✦ IN THE SIN BIN ✦

Three England players have been suspended on a single occasion from World Cup finals matches: Ray Wilkins, Terry Fenwick and Paul Gascoigne.

✦ THE EMPIRE STADIUM ✦

England played a total of 223 games at the old Wembley Stadium in 76 years from 1924 to 2000. As part of the British Championship England played the other three home countries at Wembley every other year, Scotland from the 1920s and Wales and Northern Ireland since the 1950s. Scotland paid the most visits to Wembley for an international against England with 30, then Northern Ireland with 18 visits and Wales with 16. Apart from the home countries, Brazil and Germany/West Germany were the next most frequent Wembley opposition for England with nine visits each.

✦ BORROWED SOCKS ✦

When England played Brazil in Rio de Janeiro on 8 June 1977 they wore red shirts, white shorts and blue socks. However, when England played Argentina and Uruguay in the remaining games of their 1977 South American tour they wore their usual red socks. It is believed that England arrived in Rio de Janeiro without their red socks and had to borrow a set of blue socks from their hosts.

✦ ONE HELL OF A BEATING ✦

Norway beat England 2–1 in the Ullevaal Stadium, Oslo, on 9 September 1981 in a 1982 World Cup qualifying game. After Norway's famous victory, Norwegian TV commentator Bjorn Lillelien, launched into one of the most unashamedly partisan pieces of commentary ever when he cried out: "Lord Nelson! Lord Beaverbrook! Sir Winston Churchill! Sir Anthony Eden! Clement Attlee! Henry Cooper! Lady Diana! Maggie Thatcher - can you hear me, Maggie Thatcher? Your boys took one hell of a beating! Your boys took one hell of a beating!"

✦ UNDISPUTED BRITISH CHAMPIONS ✦

England won the Home International Championship 34 times outright, more than the other home nations added together.

⚘ ENGLAND XI – LIVERPOOL ⚘

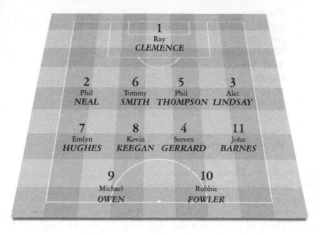

1
Ray
CLEMENCE

2
Phil
NEAL

6
Tommy
SMITH

5
Phil
THOMPSON

3
Alec
LINDSAY

7
Emlyn
HUGHES

8
Kevin
KEEGAN

4
Steven
GERRARD

11
John
BARNES

9
Michael
OWEN

10
Robbie
FOWLER

Substitutes
David *JAMES*, Jamie *CARRAGHER*, Larry *LLOYD*,
Roger *HUNT*, Ian *CALLAGHAN*
Player-Manager
Kevin *KEEGAN*

Did You Know That?
Everton played their home games at Anfield before Liverpool was even formed. Everton fell out with John Houlding, the owner of Anfield, over a proposed rent increase for the 1892–93 season. Everton moved to Goodison Park and Houlding formed Liverpool.

⚘ SHOWN THE YELLOW CARD ⚘

Terry Fenwick holds the record number of cautions for an England player at the World Cup finals tournament with three yellow cards at Mexico 1986 in the matches against Portugal, Poland and Argentina.

⚘ SHOWN THE RED CARD ⚘

Two England players have been sent off in World Cup finals play. Ray Wilkins was shown the red card for incurring two cautions against Morocco at Mexico 1986, and David Beckham for violent conduct against Argentina at France 1998.

⚜ ENGLAND'S LAST 10 POTTERS ⚜

Player	Years
Freddie Steele	1936–37
Joe Johnson	1936–37
Neil Franklin	1946–50
Tony Allen	1959
Gordon Banks	1967–72
Mike Pejic	1974
Alan Hudson	1975
Peter Shilton	1977
Dave Watson	1982
Mark Chamberlain	1982–84

Did You Know That?
Three Stoke City players have started for England on two occasions.
The first was in 1892 and the second on 17 April 1937 against Scotland
in a 3–1 defeat at Hampden Park. Stanley Matthews, Joe Johnson and
Freddie Steele all played that day, with Steele scoring for England. A
total of 22 Stoke City players have been capped by England.

⚜ THEY THINK IT'S ALL OVER ⚜

BBC sports commentator Ken Wolstenholme will always be
remembered for his famous line at the end of the 1966 World Cup
Final when Geoff Hurst scored England's fourth goal against West
Germany: "Some people are on the pitch ... they think it's all over ...
it is now!" Ken commentated on every FA Cup Final from 1953 (the
"Matthews" Final) to 1971 (Arsenal's Double year), and on five World
Cup tournaments (1954–1970) before being ousted at the BBC after
the 1970 World Cup finals to make way for David Coleman. In 1964
he became the first ever commentator on BBC's *Match of the Day*. Ken
died, aged 81, on 23 April 2002.

⚜ THE LIONS ROAR (16) ⚜

"My dream is the same as your dream, the same as all the fans and
players. That is to win a big tournament and win the World Cup."
Sven-Goran Eriksson allows himself to dream.

⚜ SVEN THE XIII ⚜

Sven-Goran Eriksson was the thirteenth person to manage England.

⚜

➤ EURO 2000 ➤

In 2000, England participated in their sixth European Championship finals which were co-hosted by Belgium and the Netherlands. At the finals, England were drawn in Group A with Germany, Portugal and Romania. England lost their opening games 3–2 to Portugal in the Phillips Stadion, Eindhoven, Netherlands. Germany, the holders, were England's next opponents and England gained revenge for their semi-final penalty shoot-out defeat of four years earlier with a 1–0 win in the Stade Communal, Charleroi, Belgium, thanks to an Alan Shearer goal. In their final group game, England lost 3–2 to the Romanians in the Stade Communal, Charleroi, Belgium, a result that left England third in the group and out of the competition.

France beat Italy 2–1 in the Final in Rotterdam with a golden goal from David Trezeguet in extra time.

FIRST ROUND, GROUP A

12 JUNE 2000, EINDHOVEN, 31,500

Portugal (2) 3   v   **England** (2) 2
(Figo 22, João Pinto 37,   (Scholes 3,
Gomes 59)   McManaman 18)

England: Seaman, Neville G., Neville P., Campbell, Adams (Keown, 82), Beckham, Scholes, Ince, McManaman (Wise, 58), Shearer, Owen (Heskey, 46).

---

17 JUNE 2000, CHARLEROI, 27,700

Germany (0) 0   v   **England** (0) 1
(Shearer 53)

England: Seaman, Neville G., Neville P., Campbell, Keown, Beckham, Scholes (Barmby, 71), Ince, Wise, Shearer, Owen (Gerrard, 61).

---

20 JUNE 2000, CHARLEROI, 27,000

England (2) 2   v   **Romania** (1) 3
(Shearer 41, Owen 45)   (Chivu 22, Munteanu 48, Ganea pen 89)

England: Martyn, Neville G., Neville P., Campbell, Keown, Beckham, Scholes (Southgate, 82), Ince, Wise (Barmby, 75), Shearer, Owen (Heskey, 67).

Group A – Final table

	P	W	D	L	F	A	Pts
Portugal	3	3	0	0	7	2	9
Romania	3	1	1	1	4	4	4
England	3	1	0	2	5	6	3
Germany	3	0	1	2	1	5	1

England's Euro 2004 Finals Squad

1	David Seaman......................(*Arsenal*)		12	Gareth Southgate......(*Aston Villa*)
2	Gary Neville.......................(*Man Utd*)		13	Nigel Martyn..........(*Leeds United*)
3	Phil Neville.......................(*Man Utd*)		14	Paul Ince..................(*Middlesbrough*)
4	Sol Campbell...........................(*Spurs*)		15	Gareth Barry..............(*Aston Villa*)
5	Tony Adams.......................(*Arsenal*)		16	Steven Gerrard.................(*Liverpool*)
6	Martin Keown.....................(*Arsenal*)		17	Dennis Wise......................(*Chelsea*)
7	David Beckham............(*Man Utd*)		18	Nicky Barmby.................(*Everton*)
8	Paul Scholes...................(*Man Utd*)		19	Emile Heskey..................(*Liverpool*)
9	Alan Shearer.........(*Newcastle Utd*)		20	Kevin Phillips...........(*Sunderland*)
10	Michael Owen.................(*Liverpool*)		21	Robbie Fowler.................(*Liverpool*)
11	Steve McManaman.....(*R Madrid*)		22	Richard Wright...(*Ipswich Town*)

Manager: Kevin Keegan

Did You Know That?
UEFA seeded four teams to head the four groups: Belgium and Netherlands as the co-host nations, Germany as the reigning European Champions, and Spain as the highest placed team in UEFA's European national team ranking table at the time of the draw in December 1999. England were ranked 17th in Europe and were placed among those teams that were seeded fourth and lowest. Only Denmark, Slovenia and Turkey at the finals had a lower UEFA ranking than England.

- ⌁ ENGLAND PLAYERS BACK THE BID ⌁ -

Arsenal's Ashley Cole joined Frank Lampard, Wayne Bridge and John Terry from Chelsea to promote London's bid to host the Olympic Games in 2012 before England's friendly game against Spain in Madrid on 17 November 2004. England eventually won the vote to host the Games.

⌁ ON HIS WAY OUT ⌁

In January 2006, Sven-Goran Eriksson announced he would be resigning after the 2006 World Cup Finals.

⚜ THE NATIONAL FOOTBALL MUSEUM ⚜

The National Football Museum is situated at Preston North End's Deepdale Stadium. It was opened on 1 December 2002 with membership open to football figures of any nationality who have made a significant contribution to the English game. The first 29 inductees comprised 22 players, six managers and one woman (Lilly Parr scorer of over 1,000 goals for Dick Kerr's Ladies team, the unofficial women's world champions in the 1920s and 1930s), and were selected from a short list of 96 nominees by a panel of 20 football experts. Since then, 34 more people have been inducted, including 23 players, 8 managers and 3 women.

The following tables list past England players and managers inducted into the National Football Museum:

Player	Inducted	Player	Inducted
John Barnes	2005	Gordon Banks	2002
Colin Bell	2005	Bobby Charlton	2002
Jack Charlton	2005	Brian Clough	2002
Ian Wright	2005	Dixie Dean	2002
Tony Adams	2004	Duncan Edwards	2002
Viv Anderson	2004	Tom Finney	2002
Geoff Hurst	2004	Paul Gascoigne	2002
Wilf Mannion	2004	Jimmy Greaves	2002
Alan Shearer	2004	Johnny Haynes	2002
Alan Ball	2003	Nat Lofthouse	2002
Stan Cullis	2003	Stanley Matthews	2002
Tommy Lawton	2003	Bobby Moore	2002
Gary Lineker	2003	Bryan Robson	2002
Stan Mortensen	2003	Peter Shilton	2002
Bill Nicholson	2003	Billy Wright	2002

Manager	Inducted
Sir Walter Winterbottom	2005
Don Revie	2004
Sir Bobby Robson	2003
Kevin Keegan	2002
Sir Alf Ramsey	2002

⚜ SVEN FOOLED BY FAKE SHEIKH ⚜

In January 2006, a *News of the World* reporter posed as a rich Arab businessman to get an interview with Sven-Goran Eriksson.

⚜ ENGLAND'S LAST 10 RANGERS ⚜

Player	Years
Dave Thomas	1974–75
Dave Clement	1976–77
John Gregory	1983–84
Terry Fenwick	1984–86
Clive Allen	1984
David Seaman	1988–90
Paul Parker	1989–91
Andy Sinton	1991–93
David Bardsley	1992–93
Les Ferdinand	1993–94

Did You Know That?

Only once have three Queens Park Rangers players ever started for England together. Gerry Francis, Ian Gillard and Dave Thomas all played in England's 2–2 draw against Wales at Wembley on 21 May 1975. Gerry Francis captained England in 1976 when they played a Team America side led by the legendary Bobby Moore. A total of 16 QPR players have been capped by England.

⚜ MOVIE STARS ⚜

Former England internationals Bobby Moore and Mike Summerbee joined then current England international Russell Osman in the 1981 movie *Escape to Victory*, directed by John Huston. In the film the Allies, all prisoners of war, agreed to play an exhibition match against local German troops in occupied Paris, only to find themselves involved in a Nazi propaganda tournament. The Allies drew with the Germans and all escaped at the end of the movie when the fans invaded the pitch. Pele, Osvaldo Ardiles and Michael Caine also starred in the movie.

Less well known is that the film was based on the true story of a group of Ukranian nationals playing under the name of Dynamo Kiev, who defeated a team of Nazi soldiers while Ukraine was occupied by Nazi troops during World War II. As a direct result of their victory over the Germans, the Ukranians were all killed.

⚜ CAPTAIN'S ARMBAND ⚜

Players inheriting the captain's armband after a substitution are not accredited "England captain" status in the official sense.

⟶ SIR TOM FINNEY, OBE ⟵

Tom Finney was born on 5 April 1922 in Preston. As a young boy Tom dreamed of becoming a professional footballer, but his father, Alf, insisted that his son should learn a trade and so Tom became an apprentice plumber. In 1940, Tom turned professional, and made his first-team debut later that year. However, Britain was then at war with Germany, and the Football League had been disbanded. During World War II, football in England was played on a regional basis and, in 1940–41, Preston won the Northern Section Championship and also reached the Final of the Wartime Cup, beating Arsenal 2–1 after a replay. It was the only final Tom ever won during his illustrious career but, sadly, wartime football honours are not recognized by the Football Association as a senior football honour. Remarkably, because of the war, Tom became one of only a small number of footballers who made their international debut before they made their full league debut for their club. Towards the end of the War he played for England in a friendly against Switzerland in Berne, but he did not get awarded a cap.

In 1942, Tom was called-up with the Royal Armoured Corps, seeing action with the Eighth Army as a tank driver and mechanic, but he still played football on the wartime guest circuit for Bolton Wanderers, Newcastle United and Southampton. On the opening day of the 1946–47, he made his much-awaited league debut for Preston against Leeds United. On 28 September 1946, Tom made his England debut scoring in a 7–2 win over Northern Ireland in Belfast. He went on to win 76 caps and score 30 goals. Of the 76 games, England lost only 12, whilst he won 50 caps before he was on a losing England side – against Scotland.

On 16 May 1948, England humiliated Italy 4–0 in Turin, with Tom scoring twice. Four years later, the Italian side, Palermo, wanted to sign Tom to help them win the Italian Championship. They offered him a £10,000 signing on fee, a wage of £130 per month, bonuses of up to £100 a game, a Mediterranean villa, a luxury car and free travel to and from Italy for his family. If he had joined them, Preston would also have been given £30,000 but he turned it all down to stay in his beloved Preston.

Tom was an extremely gifted two-footed player, who possessed an explosive shot in both feet. He was quick, had superb balance, was powerful in the air despite his size and could place a pass on a sixpence from almost anywhere on the pitch. He was never booked or sent-off. In 1961 he was awarded the OBE and, in 1998, he was knighted for his services to the game.

❧ SIR TREVOR BROOKING, MBE ❧

Trevor Brooking[†] was capped 47 times for England between 1974 and 1982, scoring five times. His most famous England goal is without doubt his second goal against Hungary in Budapest, on 6 June 1981, in a 1982 World Cup qualifying game. His long-range shot was hit so hard that it lodged against the stanchion.

❧ SUBBED OFF THREE TIMES IN A ROW ❧

Two England players have been substituted in three consecutive World Cup finals games. Bobby Charlton was taken off during the 1970 finals in Mexico in the group matches against Brazil and Czechoslovakia, and in the quarter-final against West Germany. Emile Heskey was substituted at the 2002 finals in Japan/South Korea in the group matches against Argentina and Nigeria, and in the last 16 match against Denmark.

❧ FRANK WONG SOO ❧

On 3 February 1945 Frank Wong Soo was the first player of Chinese extraction to become an England international. Indeed, Frank was the first non-white player of any ethnic background to represent England long before Viv Anderson, the first "official" black player, made his England debut on 29 November 1979. Frank was born in Buxton, Derbyshire, in 1914 and was the son of a Chinese father and an English mother. During his career he played alongside fellow England internationals Stanley Matthews and Neil Franklin at Stoke City. All three played together in the England team that faced Scotland at Villa Park on 3 February 1945. Frank won nine caps for England, but unfortunately the Football Association does not recognize appearances made during World War II.

❧ THE WEMBLEY APPEARANCE RECORD ❧

Tony Adams of Arsenal holds the record for the highest number of appearances at Wembley Stadium. He played his 60th game under the Twin Towers in England's last ever game at the old stadium, the 1–0 defeat to Germany on 7 October 2000. Tony captained England in the game.

[†]Trevor's former manager at West Ham United, Ron Greenwood, was also his manager when he played for England.

⚭ ENGLAND'S LAST 10 FOXES ⚭

Player	Years
Septimus Smith	1935
Gordon Banks	1963–67
Peter Shilton	1970–75
Keith Weller	1974
Frank Worthington	1974
Steve Whitworth	1975
Gary Lineker	1984–85
Emile Heskey	1999–2000
Steve Guppy	1999
Ian Walker	2004

Did You Know That?
Three Leicester City players – Peter Shilton, Keith Weller and Frank Worthington – all played in the same England side against Scotland and Argentina in May 1974. A total of 16 Leicester City (including Leicester Fosse) players have been capped by England.

⚭ WORLD CUP YOUNGSTER ⚭

Michael Owen is the youngest player to appear for England in the World Cup finals. He was 18 years and 183 days old when he made a substitute appearance for England against Tunisia in the opening group match of the 1998 tournament in France. Eleven days later, in England's third group match, against Colombia, Michael became the youngest player to make a starting appearance for England at 18 years and 194 days.

⚭ THE FIRST GOAL AFTER WORLD WAR I ⚭

John Cock of Huddersfield Town scored England's first goal when football resumed after World War I. Cock scored in England's 1–1 draw with Ireland in Belfast on 25 October 1919. It was Cock's international debut, and his goal is the third fastest goal scored by an England international, coming after just 30 seconds' play.

⚭ THE FASTEST EVER OWN GOAL ⚭

Bob Compton of Blackburn Rovers scored an own goal in less than one minute playing for England against Scotland in Newcastle on 6 April 1907. The game ended 1–1 thanks to a Steve Bloomer goal.

⟋ ENGLAND'S IRON MEN ⟍

Two England captains have played for Scunthope United[†]:

Ray Clemence ❖ Kevin Keegan

⟋ THE FIRST OVERSEAS PLAYER ⟍

Inter Milan's Gerry Hitchens became the first player to play for England while playing for a club side outside the UK. Gerry played and scored in England's 3–1 win at Wembley over Switzerland on 9 May 1962.[††]

⟋ HAT-TRICK HABIT ⟍

The legendary Dixie Dean was the last player to score a hat-trick for England in consecutive games[†††]:

v Belgium in Brussels on 11 May 1927 (9–1)
v Luxembourg in Luxembourg on 21 May 1927 (5–2)

⟋ ENGLAND'S FIRST NO.1 SKIPPER ⟍

Alexander Morten of Crystal Palace became the first England goalkeeper to captain the team when he led out England for only their second international at the Kennington Oval on 8 March 1873. He was a lucky omen as England beat Scotland 4–2.[††††]

⟋ THE FIRST GOAL AFTER WORLD WAR II ⟍

Horatio "Raich" Carter of Derby County scored England's first goal when football resumed after World War II. Carter scored in England's 7–2 win over Northern Ireland in Belfast on 28 September 1946. Carter had made his England debut 12 years earlier against Scotland at Wembley on 14 April 1934 when he was with Sunderland.

[†]*Ian Botham, who briefly captained the England Test cricket team, also played for Scunthorpe United.*
[††]*Joe Baker of Hibernian had scored for England against Northern Ireland on 18 November 1959.*
[†††]*Tommy Taylor scored a hat-trick against Denmark at Molineux on 5 December 1956, missed England's next game against Scotland at Wembley on 6 April 1957, and then scored his second successive hat-trick against the Republic of Ireland at Wembley on 8 May 1957.*
[††††]*Frank Swift of Manchester City became the first post-war England goalkeeper to captain the team when he led out England against Italy in Turin on 16 May 1948. England won 4–0.*

❧ WORLD CUP FINALS – KOREA/JAPAN 2002 ❧

The 2002 World Cup finals were co-hosted by Japan and South Korea. England were placed in first phase Group F along with Argentina, Nigeria and Sweden. In their opening game on 2 June, England drew 1–1 with Sweden in the Saitama Stadium, Saitama-ken, Japan. Five days later England faced bitter rivals, Argentina, in the Sapporo Dome, Sapporo City, Japan. David Beckham gained revenge for England and himself when he scored the only goal of the game from the penalty spot. In their final group game England drew 0–0 with Nigeria in the Nagai Stadium, Osaka City, Japan, a which was good enough to put England into the next stage.

On 15 June, England beat Denmark 3–0 in their second phase match in the Niigata Prefectural Stadium, Niigata-city, Japan. However, in the quarter-finals, England lost 2–1 to Brazil in the Shizuoka Stadium Ecopa, Fukuroi City, Japan. Brazil went on to win their fifth World Cup, defeating Germany 2–0 in an uninspiring Final, with both the goals scored by Ronaldo, the tournament's leading marksman.

FIRST ROUND, GROUP F

SAITAMA, 2 JUNE 2002, 52,271

England (1) *1*   vs   **Sweden** (0) *1*
(Campbell 24)   (Alexandersson 59)

England: Seaman, Mills, Cole A, Campbell, Ferdinand,
Beckham (Dyer, 63), Hargreaves, Scholes, Vassell (Cole J, 73),
Owen, Heskey.

SAPPORO, 7 JUNE 2002, 35,927

Argentina (0) *0*   vs   **England** (1) *1*
                                     (Beckham (pen) 44)

England: Seaman, Mills, Cole A (Bridge, 85), Ferdinand, Campbell,
Beckham, Scholes, Butt, Hargreaves (Sinclair, 19),
Owen (Vassell, 77), Heskey (Sheringham, 69).

OSAKA, 12 JUNE 2002, 44,864

Nigeria (0) *0*   vs   **England** (0) *0*

England: Seaman, Mills, Cole A (Bridge, 85), Ferdinand, Campbell,
Beckham, Scholes, Butt, Sinclair,
Owen (Vassell, 77), Heskey (Sheringham, 69).

Group F – Final table

	P	W	D	L	F	A	Pts
Sweden	3	1	2	0	4	3	5
England	3	1	2	0	2	1	5
Argentina	3	1	1	1	2	2	4
Nigeria	3	0	1	2	1	3	1

SECOND ROUND
NIIGATA, 16 JUNE 2002, 40,582

Denmark (0) **0**   v   **England** (3) **3**
(Ferdinand 5, Owen 22,
Heskey 44)

England: Seaman, Mills, Cole A, Ferdinand, Campbell,
Sinclair, Beckham, Scholes (Dyer, 49), Butt,
Owen (Fowler, 46), Heskey (Sheringham, 69).

QUARTER-FINAL
SHIZUOKA, 21 JUNE 2002, 47,436

England (1) **1**   vs   **Brazil** (1) **2**
(Owen 23)   (Rivaldo 45,
Ronaldinho 50)

England: Seaman, Mills, Cole A (Sheringham, 80), Ferdinand,
Campbell, Beckham, Scholes, Butt, Sinclair (Dyer, 56),
Owen (Vassell, 79), Heskey.

England's 2002 World Cup Finals Squad

1	David Seaman	*(Arsenal)*
2	Danny Mills	*(Leeds Utd)*
3	Ashley Cole	*(Arsenal)*
4	Trevor Sinclair	*(West Ham)*
5	Rio Ferdinand	*(Leeds Utd)*
6	Sol Campbell	*(Arsenal)*
7	David Beckham	*(Man Utd)*
8	Paul Scholes	*(Man Utd)*
9	Robbie Fowler	*(Leeds Utd)*
10	Michael Owen	*(Liverpool)*
11	Emile Heskey	*(Liverpool)*
12	Wes Brown	*(Man Utd)*
13	Nigel Martyn	*(Leeds Utd)*
14	Wayne Bridge	*(Southampton)*
15	Martin Keown	*(Arsenal)*
16	Gareth Southgate	*(M'brough)*
17	Teddy Sheringham	*(Spurs)*
18	Owen Hargreaves	*(Bayern)*
19	Joe Cole	*(West Ham)*
20	Darius Vassell	*(Aston Villa)*
21	Nicky Butt	*(Man Utd)*
22	David James	*(West Ham)*
23	Kieron Dyer	*(Newcastle Utd)*

Manager: Sven-Goran Eriksson

∽ WUNDERTEAM BEATEN ∾

Austria became the third foreign side to play England on English soil when the two sides met at Stamford Bridge on 7 December 1932. England narrowly defeated the "unofficial Champions of European football" 4–3. Austria were coached at the time by former Bolton Wanderers player, Jimmy Hogan.

∽ ENGLAND 4, NORTHERN IRELAND 15 ∾

When FIFA introduced their new world rankings on 14 September 2005, exactly one week after Northern Ireland's 1–0 win over England in Belfast, England dropped four places to 11th whilst Northern Ireland climbed 15 places to 101st.

∽ PROUD OF THEIR CLEAN SHEETS ∾

Gordon Banks kept a clean sheet in the first four games of the 1966 finals: the three group matches against Uruguay, Mexico and France, and England's quarter-final against Argentina, all played at Wembley Stadium, to record the most consecutive clean sheets by an England goalkeeper at the World Cup finals. Peter Shilton equalled his feat by not conceding a goal in England's last four games at the 1982 finals in Spain: the last two first-round group matches against Czechoslovakia and Kuwait, and the two second-round group matches against West Germany and Spain.

∽ BUTCH BANNED ∾

Ray Wilkins was banned[†] for two games following his two yellow cards during a 1986 group match against Morocco in Monterrey. FIFA increased the suspension from the normal one game to two because they considered his second cautionable offence to be abuse of the referee. After what he considered to be a poor decision by the referee, Wilkins tossed away the ball in disgust and it hit the referee as it bounced off the grass. It was the longest suspension for an England player in the World Cup finals.

∽ NOT ELIGIBLE FOR THE GAMES ∾

The IOC does not accept representative teams and, therefore, England are not permitted to compete at the Olympics Games.

'Wilkins' dismissal meant that he became the first England captain to be sent off.

⟶ TWO-GOAL WORLD CUP HEROES ⟵

Six England players have had two-goal games in World Cup Finals, excluding hat-tricks:

Ivor Broadis v Belgium at the 1954 tournament in Switzerland
Nat Lofthouse v Belgium at the 1954 tournament in Switzerland
Roger Hunt v France at the 1966 tournament in England
Bobby Charlton v France at the 1966 tournament in England
Bryan Robson v France at the 1982 tournament in Spain
Gary Lineker v Paraguay at the 1986 tournament in Mexico
Gary Lineker v Cameroon at the 1990 tournament in Italy

⟶ YOUNG MICHAEL OWEN ⟵

Michael Owen, then of Liverpool, came on as a substitute and scored against Romania during the 1998 Finals in France. Aged 18 years and 190 days old, he was England's youngest World Cup goalscorer.

⟶ TWO GOALS IN A MINUTE ⟵

When England beat Portugal 5–2 at Everton's Goodison Park ground on 19 May 1951, the score was 1–1 after less than 60 seconds. Bill Nicholson, of Tottenham Hotspur, put England 1–0 up within 30 seconds, only to see the Portuguese score through Patalino straight from the kick-off.

⟶ MR RELIABLE AT THE WORLD CUP ⟵

Gary Lineker scored in four consecutive World Cup finals matches. In England's last three games at the 1986 finals in Mexico he scored against Poland, Paraguay and Argentina, and in their first game of Italia '90 he found the net against the Republic of Ireland.[†]

⟶ GOD ON THEIR SIDE ⟵

Seven reverend gentlemen have played football for England: Kenneth Hunt, Beaumont Jarrett, Edward Lyttleton, John Owen, Francis Pawson, Arnold Smith and Robert Vidal.

[†]*Eight England players have scored in two consecutive World Cup finals matches: Tom Finney, Ron Flowers, Roger Hunt, Geoff Hurst, Trevor Francis, David Platt, Gary Lineker (against Cameroon and West Germany in the 1990 finals) and Michael Owen.*

~ ENGLAND XI – CHELSEA ~

1
Peter
BONETTI

2
Glen
JOHNSON

6
John
TERRY

5
John
HOLLINS

3
Wayne
BRIDGE

7
Dennis
WISE

8
Frank
LAMPARD

4
Ray
WILKINS

11
Joe
COLE

9
Jimmy
GREAVES

10
Bobby
TAMBLING

Substitutes
Dave *BEASANT*, Graeme *LE SAUX*, Terry *VENABLES*,
Peter *OSGOOD*, Kerry *DIXON*
Manager
Glenn *HODDLE*

Did You Know That?

Chelsea Football Club was founded in 1905. The club nickname
is The Blues, but they were previously known as The Pensioners.
Despite its old nickname, the club's Stamford Bridge ground is
situated outside the Royal Borough of Kensington and Chelsea.
Their ground is on the Fulham Road in Hammersmith.

~ THE LIONS ROAR (17) ~

"No one could believe it. Everyone ran up to the referee, I ran up to
him … it was just incredible that the goal was given. It's still hard
to believe."
*Peter Shilton recalls Maradona's "Hand of God" goal against England at the
1986 World Cup finals.*

~ WORLD CUP FINALS 2006 – GROUP B ~

England ❖ Paraguay ❖ Sweden ❖ Trinidad & Tobago

⌐ USEFUL MEN TO HAVE ON THE BENCH ⌐

Teddy Sheringham came on as substitute in four consecutive games at the 2002 finals in Japan/South Korea, against Argentina, Nigeria, Denmark and Brazil. Four other England players have made three substitute appearances during the last stages of the World Cup finals. Peter Beardsley was brought on as a substitute against Portugal in Mexico in 1986, and against Egypt and Cameroon at Italia '90. Steve Bull made substitute appearances at Italia '90 against the Republic of Ireland, Holland and Belgium, as did David Platt against Holland, Egypt and Belgium. Keiron Dyer made substitute appearances at the 2002 finals in Japan/South Korea against Sweden, Denmark and Brazil.

⌐ NOT THEIR FINEST HOUR ⌐

When Denmark beat England 4–1 on 17 August 2005, it was England's heaviest defeat in 25 years, since they lost 4–1 to Wales in Wrexham on 17 May 1980. When Northern Ireland beat England 1–0 on 7 September 2005, it was the first time in 25 years that Northern Ireland had scored against England.

⌐ BECKHAM SEES RED AGAIN ⌐

When David Beckham was sent off in England's 1–0 win over Austria at Old Trafford on 8 October 2005, he gained the unenviable record of becoming the first England player to be dismissed twice playing for his country.

⌐ UNDERNEATH THE ARCH ⌐

Looking across the London skyline it is impossible not to pick out the new Wembley Stadium's Arch. London's latest landmark is 133 metres high, weighs 1,750 tonnes and has a span of 315 metres. The Arch is an integral part of the stadium's design as it supports the majority of the weight of the retractable roof. The new Wembley Stadium has the biggest roof span in the world.

Did You Know That?
On 12 September 2005, the FA ordered Wembley Stadium's arch to be lit up in recognition of the England cricket team reclaiming the Ashes. Npower, sponsors of the Ashes, will also be the suppliers of electricity for the new Wembley Stadium.

∽ SIR WALTER WINTERBOTTOM, CBE, OBE ∾

Walter Winterbottom was born on 31 January 1913 in Oldham. Walter trained to be a teacher at Chester Diocesan Training College, qualifying in 1933. During his teaching career, the young Winterbotom played amateur football, and in 1936, he began his professional career with Manchester United as a centre-half. However, an injury and World War II cut his playing career short. During the 1937–38 season he suffered a spinal injury, and after just 27 games for Manchester United he retired from professional football. However, he did make wartime guest appearances for Chelsea and he played for an FA XI against a Royal Air Force XI at Luton on 6 June 1942. Never capped by England, the closest he came to playing for his country was on 10 October 1942, when he was an unused reserve in England's wartime international against Scotland at Wembley. In 1946 he was appointed national director of coaching with overall responsibility for the England team when official internationals recommenced after the war. He was appointed England team manager in May 1947, and remained in the post until Alf Ramsey replaced him in 1962. He became the first person other that the Football Association's Selection Committee to select the England team.

Walter's first game in charge of England was a 7–2 win over Northern Ireland at Windsor Park, Belfast, in the British Home International Championship on 28 September 1946. England lined-up as follows: Frank Swift (Man City), Laurie Scott (Arsenal), George Hardwick (captain – Middlesbrough), Billy Wright (Wolves), Neil Franklin (Stoke City), Henry Cockburn (Manchester United), Tom Finney (Preston North End), Raich Carter (Derby County), Tommy Lawton (Chelsea), Wilf Mannion (Middlesbrough) and Bobby Langton (Blackburn Rovers). England's goal scorers in the match were Carter, Finney, Mannion (3), Lawton and Langton.

Walter's worst moment in charge of England came at the 1950 World Cup finals hosted by Brazil. In the competition England were humiliated by the USA losing 1–0 in Belo Horizonte on 29 June 1950. On 2 November 1962, Walter took charge of England for the last time in a British Home International Championship game against Wales at Wembley Stadium. England won 4–0 with goals from Connelly, Peacock (2) and Greaves. In total, Walter Winterbottom took charge of England for 139 games and had a 56% win average. In 1963, he was awarded an OBE, a CBE followed in 1972 and in 1978 he was given a knighthood. Sir Walter Winterbottom died on 16 February 2002, aged 88.

⚜

～ ENGLAND'S LAST 10 SAINTS ～

Player	Years
David Armstrong	1982–84
Steve Williams	1983–84
Mark Wright	1984–87
Danny Wallace	1986
Alan Shearer	1992–93
Tim Flowers	1993
Matt Le Tissier	1994–97
Wayne Bridge	2002–03
James Beattie	2003
Peter Crouch	2005

Did You Know That?
Three Southampton players first played together in the same England side against Wales on 2 May 1984. David Armstrong, Peter Shilton and debutant Mark Wright all played in the 1–0 defeat in Wrexham. A total of 26 Southampton players have been capped by England.

～ ENGLAND'S TEN FASTEST GOALS ～

17 sec, Tommy Lawton v Portugal	Lisbon, 25 May 1947
27 sec, Bryan Robson v France	Bilbao 16 June 1982
30 sec, [†] John Cock v Ireland	Belfast, 25 October 1919
30 sec, [†] Bill Nicholson v Portugal	Liverpool, 19 May 1951
34 sec, Tommy Lawton v Belgium	Brussels, 21 September 1947
35 sec, Edgar Chadwick v Scotland	Glasgow, 2 April 1892
36 sec, Gareth Southgate v South Africa	Durban 22 May 2003
38 sec, Bryan Robson v Yugoslavia	Wembley, 13 December 1989
42 sec, Gary Lineker v Malaysia	Kuala Lumpar, 12 June 1991
55 sec, Geoff Hurst v Switzerland	Basle, 13 October 1971

～ WORLD CUP OLD-TIMER ～

Peter Shilton was 40 years and 295 days when he played in the third place play-off game against host nation Italy during the 1990 finals. In that game Peter won his 125th and last cap, a record for England. Stanley Matthews was 39 years and 145 days when he appeared in England's last match of the 1954 tournament, the quarter-final against Uruguay.

[†]*The goals by Cock and Nicholson were scored on their international debuts.*

⚓ EURO 2004 ⚓

The 2004 European Championship finals were held in Portugal. At the Finals, England were drawn in Group B with Croatia, France and Switzerland. England lost their opening game to France 2–1 in the Estádio da Luz, Lisbon, beat the Swiss 3–0 in the Estádio Municipal de Coimbra, and beat Croatia 4–2 in the Estádio da Luz. England finished second to France in the group and progressed to the quarter-finals where they drew 2–2 with the host nation, Portugal, with goals from Lampard and Owen before going out of the competition after losing the resulting penalty shoot-out 6–5.

Greece generated the greatest shock in European Championship history when they beat the hosts Portugal in the Final in Lisbon, with the only goal of the game scored by Angelos Charisteas after 56 minutes.

FIRST ROUND, GROUP B

13 JUNE 2004, LISBON, 65,200

France (0) 2   v   **England** (1) 1
(Zidane 90, 90)   (Lampard 39)

England: James, Neville G., Cole, Campbell, King, Beckham, Lampard, Gerrard, Scholes (Hargreaves, 76), Owen (Vassell, 69), Rooney (Heskey, 76).

---

17 JUNE 2004, COIMBRA, 28,500

England (1) 3   v   **Switzerland** (0) 0
(Rooney 23, 76,
Gerrard 83)

England: James, Neville G., Cole, Terry, Campbell, Beckham, Gerrard, Lampard, Scholes (Hargreaves, 71), Owen (Vassell, 73), Rooney (Dyer, 84)

---

21 JUNE 2004, LISBON, 57,047

Croatia (1) 2   v   **England** (2) 4
(Kovac N. 5, Tudor 73)   (Scholes 40, Rooney 46, 67,
                         Lampard 78)

England: James, Neville G., Cole, Campbell, Terry, Beckham, Gerrard, Scholes (King, 69), Lampard (Neville P., 83), Owen, Rooney (Vassell, 71).

Group B – Final table

	P	W	D	L	F	A	Pts
France	3	2	1	0	7	5	7
England	3	2	0	1	8	4	6
Croatia	3	0	2	1	4	6	2
Switzerland	3	0	1	2	1	6	1

QUARTER-FINAL

24 JUNE 2004, LISBON, 62,564

Portugal (0) 2 v **England (1) 2**

(Postiga 83, Rui Costa 110) (Owen 3, Lampard 115)

England lost 5–6 on penalties after extra time (90min: 1–1)

England: James, Neville G., Cole, Campbell, Terry, Beckham, Gerrard (Hargreaves, 81), Scholes (Neville P., 57), Lampard, Owen, Rooney (Vassell, 27).

England's Euro 2004 Finals Squad

1	David James....................*(Man City)*	13	Paul Robinson......................*(Spurs)*
2	Gary Neville.....................*(Man Utd)*	14	Phil Neville....................*(Man Utd)*
3	Ashley Cole.........................*(Arsenal)*	15	Ledley King..............................*(Spurs)*
4	Steven Gerrard ....*(Liverpool)*	16	Jamie Carrigher............*(Liverpool)*
5	John Terry...........................*(Chelsea)*	17	Nicky Butt......................*(Man Utd)*
6	Sol Campbell....................*(Arsenal)*	18	Owen Hargreaves......*(B Munich)*
7	David Beckham..........*(R Madrid)*	19	Joe Cole...............................*(Chelsea)*
8	Paul Scholes.....................*(Man Utd)*	20	Kieron Dyer.........*(Newcastle Utd)*
9	Wayne Rooney...............*(Man Utd)*	21	Emile Heskey.................*(Liverpool)*
10	Michael Owen ....*(Liverpool)*	22	Ian Walker................*(Leicester City)*
11	Frank Lampard................*(Chelsea)*	23	Darius Vassell ....*(Aston Villa)*
12	Wayne Bridge....................*(Chelsea)*		

Manager: Sven-Goran Eriksson

Did You Know That?

Greece had not won a single game at a major football championship prior to Euro 2004.

⟿ THE OLYMPIAN MARKSMAN ⟿

Vivian John Woodward won 23 caps (29 goals) for England and played 30 times for England Amateurs (44 goals). He once scored 8 goals in a 15–0 win over France in 1906. He played for Tottenham Hotspur and was the Great Britain captain at the 1908 and 1912 Olympic Games.

✣ ENGLAND PLAYERS IN TV ADS ✣

Player	Advert
David Beckham	Adidas, Brylcream, Pepsi, Police Sunglasses
Andy Cole	Reebok
Jermain Defoe	Adidas
Rio Ferdinand	Anti-Bullying Campaign, Anti-Racism Campaign, Nationwide Building Society
Paul Gascoigne	Walker's Crisps
Kevin Keegan	Brut Aftershave, Dentyne Chewing Gum, Sugar Puffs
Frank Lampard Jnr	*The Sun* (Goals pullout supplement), Tesco
Gary Lineker	Walker's Crisps
Gary Neville	Vodafone
Phil Neville	Vodafone
Michael Owen	Lucozade, Nationwide Building Society, Walker's Crisps,
Stuart Pearce	Pizza Hut
Jamie Redknapp	Nationwide Building Society
Sir Bobby Robson	Barclay's Bank
Wayne Rooney	Powerade
Alan Shearer	Braun, Lucozade, McDonalds, Continental Tyres
Gareth Southgate	Pizza Hut
John Terry	Pro Evolution Soccer 5
Chris Waddle	Pizza Hut
Ray Wilkins	Tango Orange (voiceover)

✣ SUBS MAKE THE DIFFERENCE ✣

Only two England substitutes have scored at the World Cup finals. David Platt came on for Steve McMahon after 72 minutes against Belgium at Italia '90, and scored the only goal of the game in the last minute of extra time. Michael Owen replaced Teddy Sheringham after 73 minutes against Romania at the 1998 finals in France and scored six minutes later to bring England level at 1–1, only for Romania to win the game with a goal in the last seconds.

✣ ON-OFF RELATIONSHIP WITH FIFA ✣

The FA joined FIFA in 1906. In 1920, the FA withdrew from FIFA, refusing to play Austria, Germany and Hungary. They rejoined in 1924, and then left again in 1928 following a dispute over players' payments, only to rejoin for a third and final time in 1946.

∽ ENGLAND'S FIRST 10 WINS ∾

Opponent	Date	Opponent	Date
Scotland	8 March 1873	Bohemia	13 June 1908
Wales	18 January 1879	Belgium	21 May 1921
Ireland	18 February 1882	N Ireland	21 October 1922
Austria	6 June 1908	France	10 May 1923
Hungary	10 June 1908	Sweden	21 May 1923

∽ ENGLAND'S FIRST 10 DEFEATS ∾

Opponent	Date	Opponent	Date
Scotland	7 Mar 1874	France	14 May 1931
Wales	26 February 1881	Hungary	10 May 1934
Ireland	15 February 1913	Czechoslovakia	16 May 1934
N Ireland	20 October 1923	Austria	6 May 1936
Spain	15 May 1929	Belgium	9 May 1936

∽ WORLD CUP FINALS RECORD ∾

Year	Rank	Teams	Stage Reached	P	W	D	L	F	A	GD	Pts
1930	-	-	Did not enter	-	-	-	-	-	-	-	-
1934	-	-	Did not enter	-	-	-	-	-	-	-	-
1938	-	-	Did not enter	-	-	-	-	-	-	-	-
1950	8	13	1st phase group	3	1	0	2	2	2	0	2
1954	7	16	Quarter-finals	3	1	1	1	8	8	0	3
1958	10	16	1st phase group play-off	4	0	3	1	4	5	-1	3
1962	8	16	Quarter-finals	4	1	1	2	5	6	-1	3
1966	1	16	Final	6	5	1	0	11	3	+8	11
1970	8	16	Quarter-finals	4	2	0	2	4	4	0	4
1974	-	-	Failed to qualify	-	-	-	-	-	-	-	-
1978	-	-	Failed to qualify	-	-	-	-	-	-	-	-
1982	6	24	2nd phase group	5	3	2	0	6	1	+5	8
1986	8	24	Quarter-finals	5	2	1	2	7	3	+4	5
1990	4	24	Semi-final and third place play-off match	7	3	3	1	8	6	+2	9
1994	-	-	Failed to qualify	-	-	-	-	-	-	-	-
1998	9	32	Round of 16 teams	4	2	1	1	7	4	+3	7
2002	6	32	Quarter-finals	5	2	2	1	6	3	+3	8
2006	-	32	Qualified								

⤙ WORLD CUP GOAL MACHINE ⤚

Gary Lineker is England's top World Cup Finals goalscorer with 10 goals in 12 matches. He scored six times in five games during the Mexico World Cup in 1986, and four times in seven games at Italia '90. Next comes Geoff Hurst with five goals in six games: four goals in three games at the 1966 finals and one goal in three games at the 1970 finals in Mexico.

⤙ ENGLAND'S 50 BLACK PLAYERS ⤚

Up to the end of the 2004–05 season, 50 black players have played for England in 133 years of international football.

Viv Anderson ❖ Laurie Cunningham ❖ Cyrille Regis ❖ Ricky Hill
Luther Blissett ❖ Mark Chamberlain ❖ John Barnes ❖ Danny Thomas
Brian Stein ❖ Danny Wallace ❖ David Rocastle ❖ Des Walker
Michael Thomas ❖ Paul Parker ❖ John Fashanu ❖ Ian Wright
John Salako ❖ Earl Barrett ❖ Mark Walters ❖ Brian Deane
Gary Charles ❖ Andy Gray ❖ Tony Daley ❖ Carlton Palmer
Keith Curle ❖ Paul Ince ❖ Les Ferdinand ❖ Andy Cole
Stan Collymore ❖ Sol Campbell ❖ Ugo Ehiogu ❖ David James
Rio Ferdinand ❖ Dion Dublin ❖ Wes Brown ❖ Emile Heskey
Kieron Dyer ❖ Chris Powell ❖ Ashley Cole ❖ Trevor Sinclair
Michael Ricketts ❖ Darius Vassell ❖ Ledley King ❖ Jermaine Jenas
Glen Johnson ❖ Jermain Defoe ❖ Anthony Gardner
Shaun Wright-Phillips ❖ Kieran Richardson ❖ Zat Knight

⤙ ENGLAND'S WORLD CUP HOT-SHOTS ⤚

	WCQ	WCF	Total		WCQ	WCF	Total
Gary Lineker	5	10	15	Ian Wright	7	0	7
Michael Owen	6	4	10	Nat Lofthouse	3	3	6
David Platt	7	3	10	John Barnes	5	0	5
Bobby Charlton	5	4	9	David Beckham	3	2	5
Bryan Robson	7	2	9	Geoff Hurst	0	5	5
Alan Shearer	6	2	8	Kevin Keegan	5	0	5
Tommy Taylor	8	0	8	Paul Mariner	4	1	5
Paul Gascoigne	7	0	7	Tony Woodcock	5	0	5

⤙ ENGLAND'S AC MILAN BRIGADE ⤚

Luther Blissett ❖ Jimmy Greaves ❖ Mark Hateley ❖ Ray Wilkins

⊕

⟶ ENGLAND'S LAST 10 SEASIDERS ⟵

Player	Years
Stanley Matthews	1947–57
Stan Mortensen	1947–53
Eddie Shimwell	1949
Tom Garrett	1952–53
Ernie Taylor	1953
William Perry	1955–56
Jimmy Armfield	1959–66
Ray Charnley	1962
Tony Waiters	1964
Alan Ball	1965–66

Did You Know That?
Four Blackpool players were in the starting 11 for England against Hungary on 25 November 1953 when "the Mighty Magyars" taught England a lesson, winning 6–3 at Wembley. Harry Johnston, Stan Matthews, Stan Mortensen and Ernie Taylor all played in the game. When Hungary beat England 7–1 in Budapest the following May not a single Blackpool player was on the pitch. A total of 13 Blackpool players have been capped by England.

⟶ WORLD CUP PUBS ⟵

The Famous Three Kings pub in London W14 depicts England's victory in the 1966 World Cup Final. It shows England captain Bobby Moore holding aloft the World Cup while beside him stand the comedian Tommy Cooper and the King of rock and roll, Elvis Presley. Sir Alf Ramsey has a pub named after him in Tunbridge Wells.

⟶ MAKING AN INSTANT IMPRESSION ⟵

More than 50 players have marked their international debut for England with a goal. Here is a selection of the scoring debutants:

Joe Baker ✻ Steve Bull ✻ Mark Chamberlain ✻ Bobby Charlton
Allan Clarke ✻ Les Ferdinand ✻ Paul Goddard ✻ Jimmy Greaves
Johnny Haynes ✻ Glenn Hoddle ✻ Roger Hunt ✻ David Johnson
Ray Kennedy ✻ Robert Lee ✻ Nat Lofthouse ✻ Wilf Mannion
Jackie Milburn ✻ Stan Mortensen ✻ Bill Nicholson ✻ Don Revie
Bobby Robson ✻ Alan Shearer ✻ Bobby Smith ✻ Peter Taylor
Darius Vassell ✻ Dennis Viollett ✻ Danny Wallace ✻ Dennis Wise

⌐ HE'S DAFT AS A BRUSH ⌐

There's certainly never a quiet moment when Paul Gascoigne is around. Here are some of the many pranks Gazza has got up to for club and country:

1. Gazza turned up for England training the morning after England's manager, Bobby Robson, had described him as being "as daft as a brush", with a floor brush sticking out of his socks.

2. Gazza set up his best mate, Jimmy "Five Bellies" Gardner, with a girl Gazza knew was a transvestite.

3. During his time at Middlesbrough he crashed the team bus at the club's training ground, causing £10,000 worth of damage.

4. On a trip to London, he jumped out of his car and asked a workman for "a go" on his pneumatic drill. When the bemused workman agreed, Gazza was watched by members of the public as he happily pounded the pavement.

5. When asked for his nationality before an operation, Gazza informed the nurse that he was "Church of England".

6. One hour after playing in an international for England he met up with Danny Baker and Chris Evans in a Hampstead pub. Gazza was still wearing his full kit, football boots and all.

7. Whilst at Newcastle United Gazza booked a series of sun-bed sessions for a team-mate, Tony Cunningham. Tony is black.

8. Approached by a reporter and asked for a comment whilst at SS Lazio, he burped into a television microphone. SS Lazio fined him £9,000.

9. Gazza once sent a rose to the Wimbledon dressing-room for Vinnie Jones after the infamous testicle-squeezing incident. Vinnie returned the compliment by sending Gazza a toilet brush.

10. During a Glasgow Rangers versus Hibernian game, the referee dropped his yellow card. Gazza picked it up, ran after the referee, stopped him and held the card aloft in the air as if he was booking the referee. The referee did not see the funny side and booked him!

11. On his first night in Rome after signing for SS Lazio, Gazza gave his minder the slip, went to his room and, after placing his shoes by an open window in his bedroom, hid in a wardrobe. The poor minder thought Gazza had committed suicide by jumping out the window.

12. Gazza completely shredded an Armani suit belonging to his England team-mate Dennis Wise. When asked why he did it, he replied, "For a laugh."

13. Gazza took a television documentary team to a beautiful Scottish cottage, which he told the director that he'd bought. He then pretended he'd forgotten his key and knocked on the door. An old lady appeared and Gazza told her that he was filming an advert for soap powder and wanted to know if she preferred Daz or Omo.
14. Gazza taught every one of his SS Lazio team-mates to swear in English with a Geordie accent.
15. Following his ex-wife Sheryl's breast implants operation, which he paid for, Gazza sent her a bunch of flowers at the hospital with a card addressed to "Dolly Parton".
16. When Gazza was an apprentice at Newcastle United, he took Kevin Keegan's football boots home to show off to his mates and left them on the Newcastle underground by mistake.
17. During a stay at a Scottish hotel, Gazza drove his four-wheel-drive jeep across its golf course, much to the annoyance of the golfers.
18. Gazza pretended he could speak Danish when he was introduced to the president of Denmark's Football Association. When he was then invited to say something in Danish, he imitated the Swedish Chef from television's "The Muppet Show".
19. After Italia '90, where Chris Waddle, his England team-mate from Sheffield Wednesday, starred in the finals, Gazza walked into a Sheffield barber shop and demanded "a Waddle cut".
20. When he was at Middlesbrough Gazza walked into the canteen and ordered lunch wearing nothing but his football socks.

⌁ WORLD CUP HAT-TRICK HEROES ⌁

Two England players have scored a hat-trick in a World Cup finals tournament. But Geoff Hurst is the only player from any country to score a hat-trick in the World Cup Final, which he did in England's 4–2 extra-time victory over West Germany on 30 July 1966 at Wembley Stadium. Gary Lineker became the only England player to score a hat-trick in the first 90 minutes in a World Cup finals game, when he scored all three goals in England's 3–0 group stage win against Poland on 11 June 1986.

⌁ THE LIONS ROAR (18) ⌁

"We were the world champions, which was a fantastic feeling. I knew that life for me would never be the same again."
Sir Bobby Charlton's reaction to England's 1966 World Cup triumph.

⌐ BIBLIOGRAPHY & REFERENCES ⌐

WEBSITES

www.bobbymooreonline.co.uk ❖ www.englandfanzine.co.uk
www.englandfc.com ❖ www.englandfootballonline.com
www.planetworldcup.com ❖ www.thefa.com ❖ www.uefa.com
www.ifhof.com ❖ www.ffbookmarks.com
www.andwaddlestepsup.com ❖ www.rsssf.com ❖ www.fifa.com
www.england-afc.co.uk ❖ www.fleurdelis.com ❖ www.anzowls.com
www.thisisbolton.co.uk ❖ www.phespirit.info
www.thewolvessite.co.uk ❖ www.fifaworldcup.yahoo.com
www.wembleystadium.com ❖ www.goalkeepersaredifferent.com
www.football-rumours.com ❖ www.en.wikipedia.org
www.bbc.co.uk/stoke ❖ www.cyberhymnal.org
www.news.bbc.co.uk ❖ www.nationalfootballmuseum.com
www.observer.guardian.co.uk ❖ www.geocities.com
www.dspace.dial.pipex.com ❖ www.bbc.co.uk/fivelive
www.taipeitimes.com ❖ www.givemefootball.com
www.wikipedia.org ❖ www.soccerphile.com ❖ www.everyhit.com

BOOKS

❖ *Bogota Bandit*, Richard Adamson, Mainstream Publishing.
❖ *England – The Football Facts*, Nick Gibbs, 1988, Facer Publishing Limited.
❖ *England: The Quest for the World Cup*, Clive Leatherdale, 1994, Two Heads Publishing.
❖ *A Football Compendium: An Expert Guide to the Books, Films & Music of Association Football*, second edition, compiled by Peter J. Seddon, 1999, Redwood Books.
❖ *Record Collector: Rare Record Price Guide*, Sean O'Mahony, 2002, Parker Mead Limited.
❖ *The Book of British Hit Singles & Albums (Edition 17)*, David Roberts, 2004, Guinness World Records Limited.
❖ *The Daily Telegraph Football Chronicle*, Norman Barrett, 2004, Carlton Books.
❖ *The Little Book of England*, Clive Batty, 2006, Carlton Books.